America Recovered

America Recovered

Photographs by
Chad Ress

Essays by
Jordan H. Carver
Miriam Paeslack

Foreword by
Bonnie Honig

Actar Publishers
New York, Barcelona

America Recovered

Published by Actar Publishers, New York, Barcelona
www.actar.com

Authors
Jordan H. Carver, Bonnie Honig, Miriam Paeslack, Chad Ress

Editor
Jordan H. Carver

Graphic Design
Jordan H. Carver

Copy editor and proofreader
Caitlin Blanchfield

Printing and binding
Gráficas Campás, Barcelona, Spain

Distribution
Actar D, Inc. New York, Barcelona

New York
440 Park Avenue South, 17th Floor
New York, NY 10016, USA
+1 212 966 2207
salesnewyork@actar-d.com

Barcelona
Roca i Batlle 2-4
08023 Barcelona, Spain
+34 933 282 183
eurosales@actar-d.com

Indexing
English ISBN: 9781945150937
PCN: Library of Congress Control Number: 2017962245

Printed in Spain

Publication date: September 2019

Contents

Acknowledgments

This book is the result of an intensely collaborative effort between Jordan Carver, Chad Ress, and Miriam Paeslack. The project started during a symposium held at the School of Architecture and Planning at the University at Buffalo. Jordan had been appointed the 2014–2015 Peter Reyner Banham Fellow and the symposium, "The Aesthetics of Citizenship," was the culmination of a year of teaching and research into the relationship between aesthetic practices, political action, and the performance of citizenship. A sincere thank you to all of the participants from that day: Jordan Geiger and Hadas Steiner from the University at Buffalo, Keller Easterling from Yale University, Jonathan Soloman from the School of the Art Institute of Chicago, Stacey Clarkson James from *Harper's Magazine*, and Christina P. Orsi from Empire State Development.

This project would not have been possible without the support of the University at Buffalo, the unique opportunity presented by the Peter Reyner Banham fellowship, and the unwavering confidence of Dean Robert Shibley and Architecture Chair Omar Khan. "The Aesthetics of Citizenship" was organized by Jordan, included work by Chad, and was attended by Miriam. The common link between the three is Stacey Clarkson James. Stacey has worked with Chad for years as the Art Director of *Harper's Magazine*. She enthusiastically presented his work at the symposium, and it was a conversation between her, Jordan, and Miriam that initiated this book.

America Recovered was funded by grants from the New York State Council for the Arts (NYSCA) and the New York University School of Social and Cultural Analysis. Thank you to NYSCA and to Jennifer Morgan at NYU.

Jordan would like to thank Jess Ngan for an amazing year in Buffalo and supporting me in every way. Thanks to Omar Khan, Hadas Steiner, Jordan Geiger, Miguel Guitart, and all of my studio and seminar students for helping me think through these ideas in a more intelligent way. Thank you to Mabel O. Wilson, Felicity D. Scott, Mark Wasiuta, Andrew Ross, Nikhil Pal Singh, Cristina Beltrán, and Thuy Linh Tu. Thanks to Jacob Moore for his pointed criticism and insight regarding my essay. To Caitlin Blanchfield for her keen eye in copyediting, proofreading, and much more. Thank you to Ricardo Deseva at Actar. To Bonnie Honig for her brilliant foreword. And thank you to Chad Ress and Miriam Paeslack for such a wonderful experience.

Chad wishes to thank his wife Stephanie, for her support and dedication through the many years it took to see this project come to fruition. To Richard and Cissy Ross, for providing their considerable journalistic experience and early encouragement. Your advice was, and is, instrumental in forging a clear path forward. My sincerest gratitude to Stacey Clarkson James, who nurtured the project from its early stages and contributed greatly to not only to its expansion, but also my photographic career writ large. Your commitment is invaluable. James Welford, for his deep understanding, inspiration and seemingly endless availability. I am indebted to Jordan Carver, who not only wrote a masterful essay for this project, but also for contributing his vast skill set in many other areas as well. Above all, you have been a welcome and dedicated partner throughout, whose ongoing efforts accumulated directly to the publishing of the book held here. Miriam Paeslack for contributing her significant understanding of the photographs through an essay which so succinctly ties together many narrative threads. Bonnie Honig for her introduction which adds such a necessary viewpoint and reminds us of the value of the common good. There are many others I would like to thank for their help and support including Deric and Barbara Washburn, Ricardo Devesa, Gregory Rodriguez, Jonathan Feldman, John Houck, John Walsh, The City of Detroit, The Army Corps of Engineers, Rebecca Horne, Ian Volner, Andrew Hinderaker, my parents, and Albert Camus for reminding me that we must imagine Sisyphus happy. And lastly to my son Cyrus, who constantly reminds me of what is important in life.

Miriam would like to thank Francesca Russello Ammon who invited her to present early thoughts about Ress's work at the symposium "Picturing Policy: How Visual Culture Shapes the Urban Built Environment," at the University of Pennsylvania, April 2016; Mary Woods and Anne Whiston Spirn for their critical feedback at the symposium. Jordan Geiger as critical reader and editor; Jacob Moore and Caitlin Blanchfield for their wonderful editorial work.

The Beauty of Public Things

Bonnie Honig

Is nostalgia more tempting these days than it once was? It is certainly hard not to view this book's incredible project of American "recovery" through a nostalgic lens. The website Recovery.gov charted the Obama-era effort to combat the 2008 economic recession with a stimulus strategy of large-scale public investment in infrastructure. Engagingly sampling that effort, *America Recovered* creates a record of it, and reminds us of the importance of infrastructure to collective, democratic life and of shared public imagery to democratic imagination, courage, and collaborative self-governance.

It is impossible to look at this book's pictorial documentation of the American Recovery and Reinvestment Act (ARRA) and not think of the famous Work Projects Administration (WPA) projects and images that knitted together parts of a nation after the Depression and still, to this day, inspire wonder. The much-photographed monumental WPA dams stand out, fittingly, since the WPA seemed to underwrite its confidence in the power of the nation to steer the economy precisely by celebrating the human power to leash even nature to our purposes. Our hubris on the latter front has since been chastened, but it is survived for many by the still ambitious idea that government does have a welcome role to play in inspiring and securing collective action for common cause. It was this idea, surely, that motivated Barack Obama to say, during his first presidential campaign, that he wanted to "make government cool again." It is also what motivates the remarkable textual and photographic essays collected in this book.

Two differences between the WPA and the ARRA stand out in the stark relief of Chad Ress's images: The ARRA, with its focus on shovel-ready projects, many of which had been on hold for lack of available funding in an era of lowered taxation and public disinvestment, tended to promote the local not the national and the piecemeal rather than the grand plan. Perhaps as a result, what we see in *America Recovered* are often scenes of democratic disrepair and abandonment. Are these the dystopic remains of the New Deal's once ambitious vision to render real through infrastructure the imagined community of a democratic form of life?

The second difference is this: where the WPA funded photographers to record and publicize the program's great works, the ARRA went largely unpublicized. As Jordan Carver notes in his essay, this was likely due to partisan complaints, like California Republican Darrell Issa's, about the Obama administration's use of signs and a website to promote awareness of the work of recovery. Issa claimed these public communications were evidence of the President's failure "to transition from campaign-mode to leadership-mode." They were in fact exactly the opposite, part of a presidential team's effort to lead the country on the verge of catastrophe by addressing an economic emergency via public spending and democratic accountability. But the Republican critique had its effects.

Thus, especially after the 2010 midterms, preserving the ARRA meant keeping it quiet. The ARRA would be allowed to stimulate the economy only if it did not also stimulate the senses. And yet democracies cannot thrive without the sensory stimulation of public things. If a solar energy project is built in the woods and no one is there to hear it, will it make a sound? It may generate energy for use, but it will not generate the affective civic ties among those who, in concert, are able to build what no one of them could do alone: a public thing.

Public things are not only instrumental providers of certain goods, like electricity for use or jobs for earnings. They also serve a larger constitutive purpose. They are part of the "holding environment" of democratic citizenship, the objects of a common world, cared for in common. They gift us with their stability and relative permanence. They are both architectural and imagistic, including national parks, schools, sewage plants, prisons, transportation infrastructure, dams, archives, films, and more. They press us into debate and force us to sort out our differences, or to agree to disagree, or to mobilize better the next time. They furnish the world of democratic life and, just like furniture in a home, they help us keep our bearings, provide us with fixed points of stability as we, sometimes dizzyingly, coordinate or conflict with others who are like *and* unlike us. The political theorist, Hannah Arendt, coined the phrase "action in concert" for this definitive experience of democratic life. She saw such action as part of a practice of world-building in which we pursue our collective interest. And, as she pointed out, interest literally means being among others: *inter-est*.

One of my favorite examples of a public thing that positions us *inter-est* predates both the ARRA and the WPA. It is New York City's Central Park. Built in an awful swamp, the Park is a great figure for public things, which need not be cheap in order to be common, and can in fact be quite grand. Built by laborers and craftsmen with incredible skills, and using lavish materials, Central Park promised to ennoble its visitors and they in turn would later ennoble it. In particular, the park's Alhambra style tiles, whose colors do not fade out because they do not stop at the surface but run all the way through, stand as a great metaphor for public things whose power can run all the way through us so that neither they nor we fade out. No doubt, a trace of this grand idea may be what attaches a certain President to his Wall. But the aim of Central Park was not division but intersection, not to keep people out but to bring them in. Its designer, Frederick Law Olmsted, saw Central Park as a way to put to rest an old aristocratic critique of democracies, which were said to be incapable of greatness. The park would democratize beauty, he thought. Since it is a *park*, though, it also democratizes leisure: free and open to the public, the park offers to all classes and all comers the improbable opportunity to enjoy nature in the city, to find right there in its midst respite from the demands of urban life. What could be more democratic than that?

Is it an accident that in order for the park to be built, those with the imagination to envision it had also to "drain the swamp"?

While it is tempting to blame the loss of devotion to public things in the last thirty to forty years on neoliberalism's economistic preference for privatization and disinvestment, there is in the American context something else also at work (as there was also in the Republican opposition to Obama and the ARRA): race. In the United States, what is called "public" is sometimes white, sometimes black; it is rarely both. Public housing has one racial connotation; public pools, before they were desegregated, another. Notably, it was only after public pools were desegregated that *private* pools became popular among whites, and suburban houses in dominantly white neighborhoods were built with private pools in their backyards. In short, the public things of America's democracy have been part and parcel of a regime of white supremacy in which equal access to public things—accommodations, travel, parks, streets, and more—is denied to people of color. When equal access to public things is demanded and won by minorities, then the response of the majority in the US is often to abandon the public. White flight is not just from the urban to the suburban; it is from the public to the private thing.

The last few decades' evacuation of the public and its degradation are the products of a perfect storm of white supremacy and neoliberalism combined. And the result has been the weathering of democracy, which cannot survive intact without public things. Without them, action in concert is disoriented, and the signs and symbols of democratic life are devitalized. If we divest democratic states or publics of their ownership of or responsibility for public things, we reduce democratic citizenship to repetitive (private) work and exceptional (public) emergencies.

The gift of this volume is its refusal to yield to the weather of privatization, its rejection, in fact, of the idea that privatization is like the weather—"nothing you can do about it!" On the contrary, we can champion public things with the understanding that they are sites of attachment that underwrite everyday citizenships and democratic sovereignties. I think this—and not their monumentalism—is what so many people still find moving about the WPA photographs: the audacity of hope that those images telegraph to us from almost a century ago. The trace of that audacity is in the bold words and images of *America Recovered*, which not only charts one past recovery—the nearly silenced steps taken after 2008 to recover from economic catastrophe—but also hopefully conjures another.

But the future may surprise us. It may not look quite like the past. Audacity now may be enacted through new styles of citizenship more like a swarm or a multitude than like the heroic, muscular workers whose images, inspiring to so many almost a century ago, still inspire to this day. What Jordan Carver calls the "infrastructural sublime" may give way to a democratic beautiful, a smaller scale inspiration that stimulates our senses but does not stop us in our tracks and

take our breath away. There may, indeed, be reason to prefer
the beautiful to the sublime. The sublime is said to disturb,
the beautiful (merely) to please. But at their best, democracy's
small pleasures do both. The sight of workers enjoying a day
off in Central Park was once surely disturbing to some. It may
have struck others as sublime.

Perhaps, then, the photographs in this book, which
are surely an elegy to the once great sublimity of democracy,
should be seen not as an effort to reclaim that past but as an
invitation to open a different politics on the smaller scale of
the beautiful. Instead of the lost glory of the former's dystopic
remains, we may see in Ress's images the future glory of action
in concert's not-yet: an America-to-come in which democratic citizens of all races, classes, sexualities, and genders
work together for peace, equality, and justice, in large and
small scale collaborations, while also enjoying together some
leisure—perhaps even idling in the beautiful shade of their
democracy's public things.

From the Infrastructural Sublime to Not Interesting Enough

Jordan H. Carver

In a line item entry on Recovery.gov, the now-defunct website originally created to track how funds from the American Recovery and Reinvestment Act of 2009 was spent, a project in Michigan was titled, "Seeds, Sleeping Bear Dunes, Empire, Michigan." The small bit of explanatory text elaborated, "Northwest Michigan Youth Conservation Corps will work with park personnel to repair 15 miles of deteriorating hiking trails at Sleeping Bear Dunes National Lakeshore. Trails will be brushed, tread surfaces repaired and erosion control devices cleaned, repaired, and installed. Amount funded by Recovery Act: $50,000.00."

This same website entry was used by Chad Ress as a type of instruction and future caption to his corresponding photograph of a sand dune in the Sleeping Bear Dunes National Lakeshore, a coastal recreation area administered by the US Park Services outside Traverse City on Michigan's west coast. The dune appears several stories high, perhaps thirty or forty feet. Two visitors sit at the base of the sandy hill in folding lawn chairs while others walk up it, and still more can be seen standing on top, underneath a hazy, cloudless sky. The dune looks as if it has been dumped upon the earth from on high, sand flows down its side and mixes with patches of green grass at its base. The title and caption of the photo, taken directly from Recovery.gov, allude to the dune's purpose for erosion mitigation while also providing a space for recreation. The visitors in the image are wearing t-shirts and shorts and the many footsteps running up and down allude to the dune's popularity.

While the composition of the image presents a sweeping scene that expands beyond the edges of the frame, the subject is decidedly un-heroic if read against the popular discourses established by previous government stimuli and the images

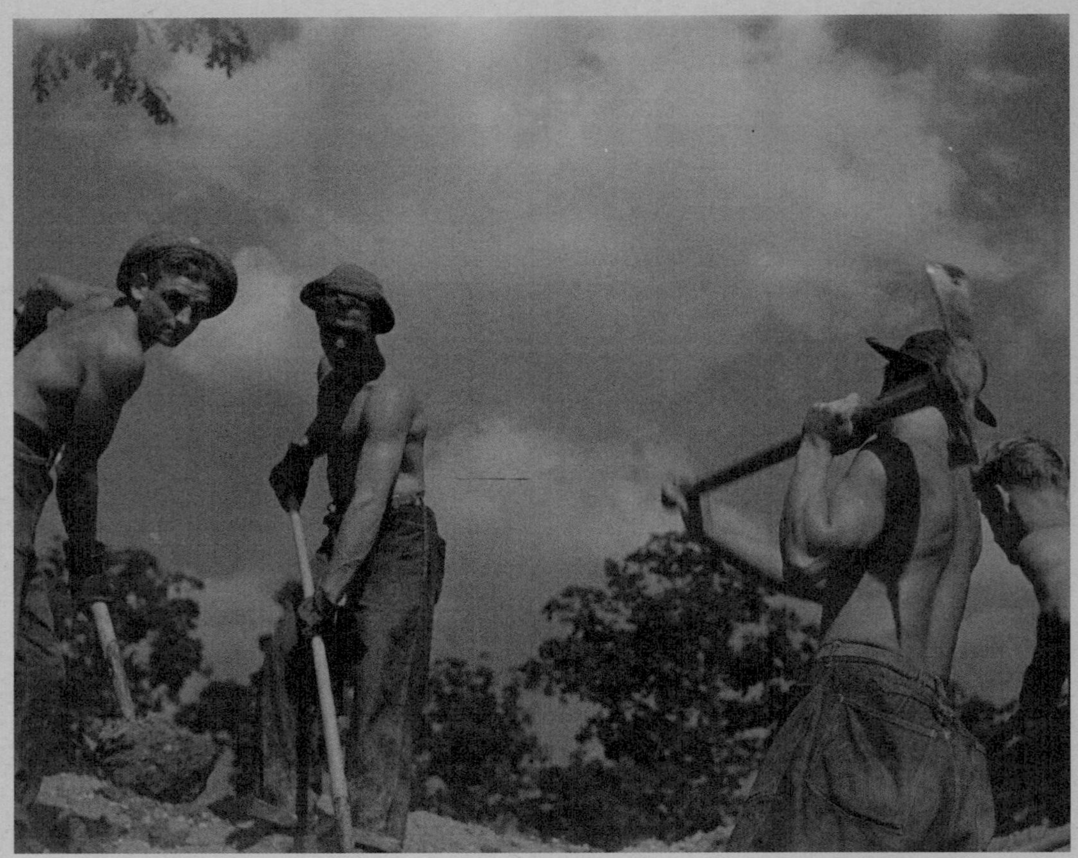

Civilian Conservation Corps "boys at work," Prince George's County, Maryland, 1935. Photograph by Carl Mydans.

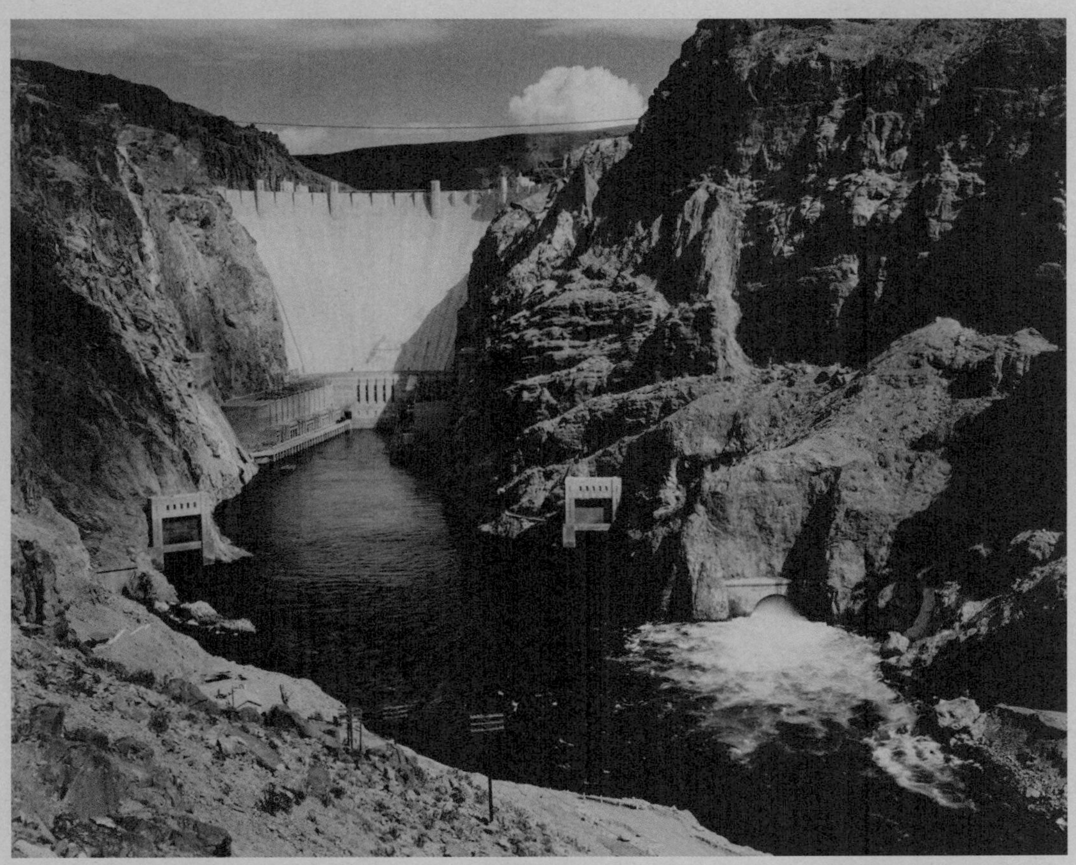

Boulder Dam, Nevada. Completed in 1936 by the Bureau of Reclamation of the Department of the Interior with $38,000,000 contributed by the Works Progress Administration. Photograph by Ansel Adams.

made to document them. Iconic examples of the genre include images of "boys at work" from the Civilian Conservation Corp and, as Miriam Paeslack more thoroughly describes, Margaret Bourke-White's innaugural *Life* magazine cover of the Works Progress Administration-funded Fort Peck Dam. The fact that the site is, by definition, for recreation does little to mark the project as a principle vehicle for infrastructural grandeur or economic recovery. The dune and its reseeding are not the type of large scale building projects traditionally conjured by politicians to sell public works and the funds required to build them. And the people photographed scaling them have little in common to the images of New Deal workers constructing a nation. While the comparison to America's most celebrated moment of physical nation-building might be unfair or overly rhetorical, it is clear that the people in Ress's photo are enjoying the land, not toiling upon it. And while the dune spread across the shore may be a striking feature upon the landscape, the Hoover Dam it is not.

The Infrastructural Sublime

"You can't build the Hoover Dam twice," claims critic Ian Volner commenting on both the physical and political legacy of the 2009 stimulus package in *Harper's Magazine*.[1] Acknowledging that the stimulus funds did not lead to any infrastructure projects that approached the grandiosity, cultural significance, or sheer environmental imprint of the Hoover Dam, Volner's statement captures the popular discourse (or lack thereof) surrounding one of President Barack Obama's early legislative accomplishments and chief domestic policy victories. Discussions around the program were largely condi-

tioned by partisan posturing and a formal invisibility due, in part, to the political, logistical, and economic environment surrounding the types of projects funded by the bill. In other words, there wasn't a singular grand plan—no network of dams, no interstate highway system, no mass housing, no stadia or city halls—that could be pinned to the stimulus package so as to whip political and popular support for its passage and success.

The American Recovery and Reinvestment Act, known more broadly as the Recovery Act, or simply the stimulus bill, was passed by the Obama administration in response to the 2008 financial crisis. The bill released $831 billion into the economy in an attempt to reverse the so-called Great Recession Obama inherited.[2] Comparisons between the Recovery Act and the New Deal were made almost immediately.[3] And writing in retrospect, reporter Michael Grabell claims the stimulus bill was the "biggest economic recovery plan in history."[4] Similarly, journalist Michael Grunwald describes the stimulus bill and Obama's economic legacy as the "New New Deal."[5]

However, questioning the lasting cultural, developmental, and infrastructural impact of the 2009 stimulus package, Volner's statement recalls a key question surrounding one of Obama's chief domestic policy victories: What, exactly did the 2009 stimulus package do? Not, "did it save the American and/or global economy?" but how did it change the country? Did it provide useful, recognizable infrastructure? Did it forever (or at least for a while) shape our cities? What, in essence, did it look like?

Volner's reference to the Hoover Dam can be read in several ways. As a spectacular feat of governmental and environmental engineering, it gave possibility to a populous desert southwest, suburban expansion, and the excesses of Las Vegas—the most American of cities. Alternatively, the dam holds a vaunted position within the collective imaginary of American ingenuity and brute force. The Hoover Dam proposes a type of welfare-state possibility and creates a visual vocabulary for marking public works and the distribution of public funds. Importantly, the dam stands as a material instantiation of the federal government, one that thinks big and is willing to invest in large-scale infrastructure and the labor required to produce it. The dam's scale is a spectacular reminder of American state-making (both bureaucratically and territorially) at the nascent stage of America's global dominance. The dam, and its heroic images, made the American state visible on a broad popular and political register. It gave American citizens and subjects of the state an image of what early twentieth century America could and should be doing, and what it could and should look like. It could be argued that without the major infrastructure projects of the era stitching together a nationalist social imagination and providing networked services to the country, America's post-World War II ascendance would be much less assured.

The dam has come to stand in for the *idea* of government stimulus and infrastructural development in general and the New Deal in particular. And the New Deal has come to stand in for an idealized conception of government stimulus and the best-case possibilities of the American welfare state. Sociologist Robert Leighninger claims it might only be a "slight" exaggeration to say "that there is hardly a community or a citizen in the country who has not benefited from the facilities" developed during the New Deal era.[6] Judging the New Deal as universally beneficial is a contested claim. Historian George Lipsitz has written of lasting racial segregation and employment inequality due to New Deal housing and welfare policies. But Leighninger is likely correct in that the architectural legacy of New Deal projects can be noted throughout the country.

During the 1930s and early 40s, many agencies and initiatives under the New Deal umbrella including the Works Progress Administration (WPA), the Public Works Administration (PWA), the Civilian Conservation Corps (CCC) and the Civil Works Administration (CWA) managed the development and construction of projects including public parks, pools, civic buildings, public services and utilities, bridges, tunnels, educational buildings, military installations, hospitals, and courthouses. A report from the WPA claims that over 40,000 building were constructed and 85,000 improved under its watch.[7] The New Deal programs quite literally built the country, establishing public spaces and institutions, and connecting them through transportation infrastructure and communication networks.

Architect Paul Cret, who designed many New Deal Projects, defines the style of the era as "WPA moderne," referring to its aesthetics as "starved classicism" or "Greco-Deco," a stylistic combination of Greco-Roman classicism and art deco futurism. Less inspirational in tone, historian Phoebe Cutler calls the New Deal style "government rustic," a type of institutional form pointing towards a frontier aesthetic marked by the prospect of western expansion.[8] Regardless of the genre or aesthetic category, these stylistic designations signal that architects and historians have decided there is *some* style or formal approach with which to group and describe the public works of the New Deal era and that aesthetics itself has played an important role in the "visibility" of the New Deal as a political project.

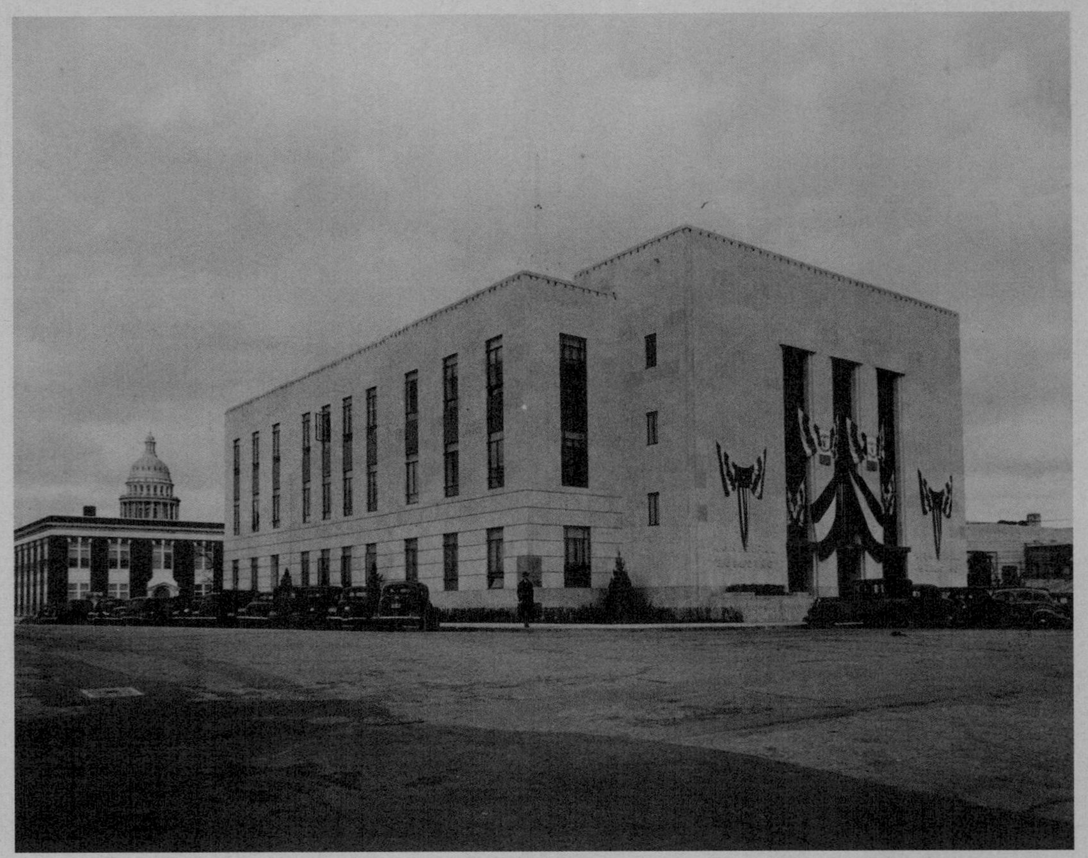

Municipal Building, Austin, Texas. Completed in 1939 with $240,768 contributed by the Works Progress Administration. Photographer unknown.

Read through the photographic media of the day, populated by towering public buildings and courageous men at work, the aesthetic style denotes an infrastructural sublime, an affective quality linking the vast scale of large infrastructural development—both in its size and the effort required to build it—with the overwhelming power of a state that could successfully accomplish such feats. The infrastructural sublime can be understood as an amalgam of David Nye's various American sublimes—the technological, the geometrical, the industrial, the electrical—but foregrounded by the status of the state as the producer of *shared* infrastructure. In this sense, the infrastructural sublime takes Nye's charge that the sublime can "weld society together" and posits a collective aesthetic experience as foundational to producing a shared politics. In the case of New Deal public works, their affective aesthetic experience forged a politics in support of spending programs and the government that passed them.[9] Like the Burkean sublime, many of the projects from the era are immense in ambition, obscure in purpose, and of such a scale their totality cannot be easily comprehended. That is, the mediated representation of New Deal projects offer a version of state power and presence, as both physical object and as image, while denying the messy and contested reality of its politics and everyday life.

The aesthetics of government infrastructural projects take on another valence when linked to the large swaths of bureaucratic energy and citizen labor required to construct them.[10] The government is itself a far-reaching and powerful entity that operates as an abstraction in terms of its power to mobilize a workforce and enact policy (this same abstraction, or distance between subject and state is often noted when the government fails to act or gets stuck within its own bureaucratic machinations). The direct line between subject —citizen, resident—and state is obfuscated and abstracted through layers of bureaucracy, taxation, and political ideology. In the case of the Recovery Act, government stimulus serves as one specific mediating object situated between subject and the state in that it represents state action and ideology in physical form. Stimulus projects stand in as material and formal manifestations of the abstract state—concrete evidence of taxpayer funding and the collective financial and political participation of the population. In the case of the New Deal and the stimulus package, the built works represent the state responding to crisis through the construction of the nation. Which is to say, one of the primary ways a citizen or state subject interacts with their government is through the use of public spaces and public institutions—whether they be libraries, national parks, courts, or prisons.

Yet if the New Deal's 40,000 new buildings made a significant spatial imprint on the country, it was arguably these buildings' photographic representations that secured the programs celebrated place within the national imagination. Forming an impressive archive produced alongside the built works through a type of employment program for out of work photographers and artists, the widely circulated images of construction projects and people at work added a visual analog to the myth of the developing state. Whether simple documentation or state propaganda, these images are marked by the sublime authority of the state and its ability to activate a citizen labor force to complete large-scale public works.

In the intervening years, New Deal programs have come to stand in for the American version of a liberal state. As historian Robert Self writes, the era's liberalism meant a "modified" welfare state, with redistribution in favor of a largely white, segregated middle class alongside aspirations for racial equality, and an individualist ideology that de-emphasized group politics.[11] The beneficial aspects of welfare state policies were sold as broad based and universal, but in application they often codified racial difference and individual rights at the expense of social and civil rights. Images of young white men from the Civilian Conservation Corps and photos of newly built public spaces deny the reality of racial segregation reinforce the romanticized history of New Deal programs. The images are coded with a racial and economic narrative that reinforces the impossibility of full equality while at the same time establishes a mythologized representation of "America." The spatio-photographic representation of the New Deal presents a significant visual benchmark to which government outlays after the New Deal have been (and will likely continue to be) judged, both in terms of architectural design and building development *and* the imagery by which such projects circulate and are consumed.

Seventy years later, the 2009 stimulus bill was signed into law and quickly contextualized within the history of New Deal state-making. The bill introduced more than $100 billion into "shovel ready" construction projects: those that had been previously planned and were either left dormant due to the recession or were already existing and could benefit from public monies. With Vice President Joe Biden standing behind him at the Denver Museum of Nature and Science, President Obama signed the Recovery Act on February 17, 2009. According to Obama, the goal of the bill was to revive the economy by "Making supplemental appropriations for job preservation and creation, infrastructure investment, energy efficiency and science, assistance to the unemployed, and State and local fiscal stabilization, for the fiscal year ending September 30, 2009, and for other purposes."[12] Obama alluded to the grandiosity of the interstate highway system and promised funds for a broad array of civic projects but kept his focus on economic growth, financial security, and the promise of jobs. If there were any desired effects for stimulus funds to increase public engagement or revive the country's civic institutions, they were conspicuously absent from the legislation's text or his administration's public relations strategy.

Funds from the bill were quickly distributed across the government, earmarked for agricultural and rural development, military construction, homeland security, state grants, unemployment assistance, and other forms of fiscal relief. House minority leader John Boehner and other Republican leaders strongly argued against the bill—most favoring only tax cuts—while left-leaning economist Paul Krugman claimed it was too small and should be increased to at least $1 trillion.[13]

The "shovel ready" imperative meant there was no large-scale strategic plan or spectacular series of projects for the administration to highlight. Nothing could stand in as an archetypical example of what the stimulus package claimed to represent. Nor was the bill sold on a broad public level, and later, when projects were complete, they weren't presented as examples of the bill's success. Furthermore, the stimulus bill contained no funds specifically marked for artists, writers, photographers, or even bureaucrats to document it's collected projects. If one feature of the New Deal was to enshrine a type of political and visual legacy, both through transforming the built environment and the image-making programs created to document these transformations, the stimulus package contained neither.

In the language of Jacques Rancière, there was no potential for visibility embedded into the legislative language of the stimulus bill. With the highly partisan environment surrounding the bill's passage, and its stated purpose for alleviating a crisis, documenting the projects' potential success wasn't considered within its scope. There were no "aesthetic practices" established to disclose and make visible the bill's interventions on the landscape in a way that was "common to the community."[14] This is not to say that the individual projects lacked aesthetic qualities, or that the projects were not documented through websites and the bureaucratic tools of spreadsheets and databases, but that as a whole, they didn't embody a cohesive aesthetic strategy readily legible to a community or population, even one as contested and fragmented as "the public."

Rancière links politics and aesthetics together through the mechanism of visibility as a mediating factor that reinforces certain power structures. Politics, for Rancière "revolves around what is seen and what can be said about it, around who has the ability to see and the talent to speak, around the properties of space and the possibilities of time."[15] By applying Rancière's understanding of politics coming from aesthetic experience, the stimulus bill's invisibility meant the bill and its policy implications could not enter into a broader political discourse. However, even if the aesthetic incoherence of the stimulus projects hinders their ascension into the theater of politics, it is not to say the stimulus projects were not marked as political in different ways.

Many of the funded transportation projects—roads, bridges—were advertised by signage designating the project as paid for by the American Recovery and Reinvestment Act. Not necessarily an aesthetic or stylistic marker of the stimulus' lasting visual impact, the signs nevertheless drew the attention of the House Committee on Oversight Government Reform and its chairman, California Republican Darrell Issa. In a report issued by the committee titled *Analysis of the First Year of the Obama Administration: Public Relations and Propaganda Initiatives*, Issa claims, "the signs provide no relevant traveler information—they are purely intended for propaganda purposes."[16] It would be easy to dismiss Issa's claim as mere partisanship or even government accountability, but beyond the partisan-political dimensions of whether or not highway signage is a form of propaganda, the claim illustrates how politics is a battle over the means and methods of visibility. In Issa's conservative point of view, government should be limited, therefore the role of government funding in infrastructure building should be hidden. Allowing the federal government to claim any credit for the potential benefits from stimlus-funded projects would directly contradict conservative dogma that the government is a poor administrator of public services.

Representative Issa and his committee also took issue with the website established by the bill that tracked how stimulus funds were spent. Recovery.gov, stated its purpose as the "government's official website providing easy access to data related to Recovery Act spending and allowing for the reporting of potential fraud, waste, and abuse."[17] Conversely, Issa, concluded the site "multiplies the Administration's investment in promoting the impact of the stimulus by effectively funneling federal dollars through state and local governments to finance propaganda material."[18] Issa's claim dissolves accountability into propaganda and underscores the question of whether or not transparency, or at least access to data and information, plays an important function in democratic governance.

As a nod to public accountability, Recovery.gov compiled a database of basic recovery project information that

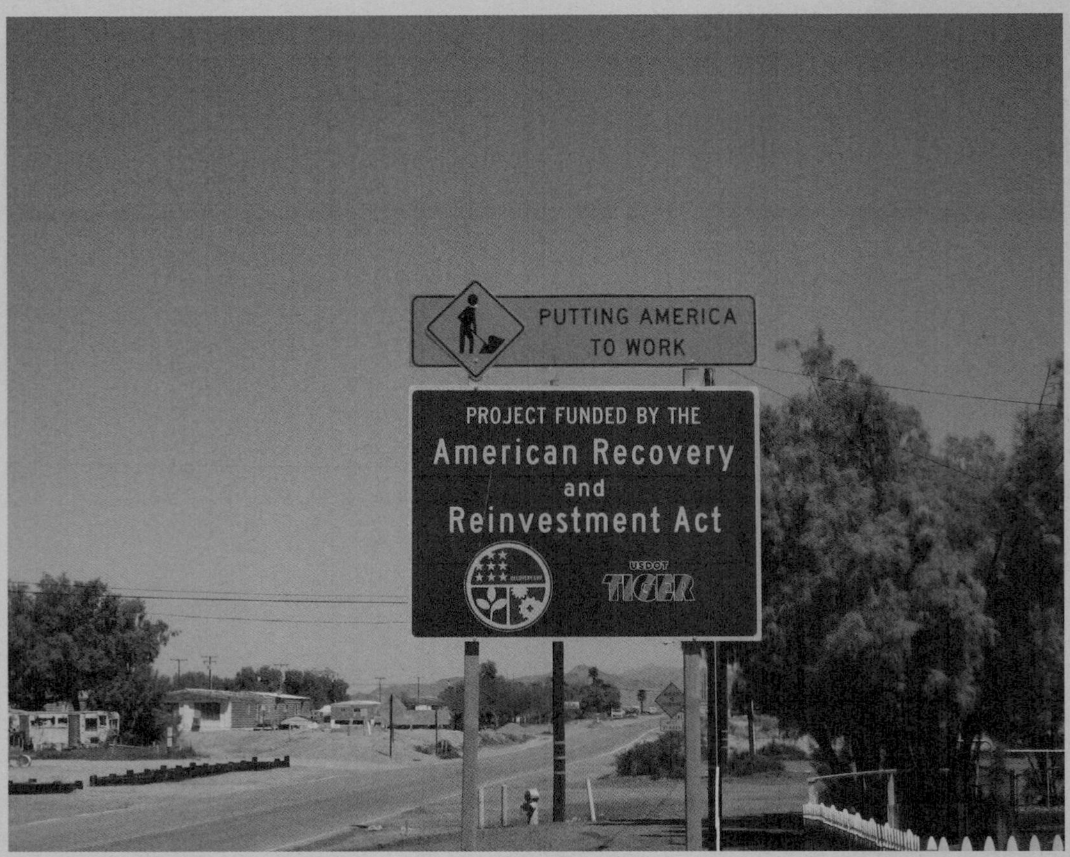

American Recovery and Reinvestment Act road sign, Baker, California, 2010. Photographer unknown.

was categorized by grant amount, governing administration, date, recipient, and a brief description of what the funds accomplished.[19] The spreadsheet and database format conformed to the site's technocratic purposes: to make data available for any individual person, government watchdog group, or academic researcher willing to parse it for their own particular purpose. Containing the stimulus bill's funding outlays within the narrow confines of the website's particular form of documentation and transactional accountability, the question of whether or not the bill was "working" continued to be refracted through political ideology—as seen explicitly in the Issa report. Political Scientist Suzanne Mettler writes that the bill was so large yet so vague and complicated that most Americans were unaware of how it would affect them, even though most received, at the very least, tax benefits due to its passage.[20] In essence, like most legislation, the bill was a large bureaucratic initiative and it was legislated without explanation or publicity. At the time of its passage the Republican-controlled Congress had an interest in making sure the bill contained no documentary requirements that could stand as evidence to the programs' utility, thus making the stimulus invisible to the broader public.

The same database and website questioned by Issa was the source document Ress used as the foundation for *America Recovered*. By combing through the Recovery.gov, Ress adopted individual project funding titles and descriptions as both prompts for and future captions to his photographic images. "The conceptual framework of this project" Ress writes, "is to reveal the point where abstract political processes manifest themselves in the physical world, thus providing an alternate means of experiencing the contemporary American landscape."[21] Ress understood that the stimulus bill would

have analogs in the physical world and the only platform created to track and describe the bill's progress displayed project information in the format of spreadsheets and online databases—textual information.

For Ress, the physical reality of the bill was hidden behind two different forms of abstraction. The first was the institutional nature of representative government; any visual or aesthetic representation of the government is by its very constitution abstract, with all interactions between citizen and government mediated through various forms of representation, whether that be website accountability or electoral politics. The second being another form of abstraction intentionally designed by political processes that either deny visual repre-sentation—Issa's strategy—or let it exist as a bureaucratic dataset. *American Recovered* is thus a deeply political project in that Ress is attempting to make visible the material forms of government spending. In doing so, he is questioning the way in which the federal government creates a subjective public. More directly, Ress's images ask what it means to be a citizen or subject of the state today—and how would we know if we are or not? As a viewer, the implied question is, what do you see? Simple road repaving, or the state in action? Rendering the stimulus through photography, Ress is prompting the viewer to make a political judgment not only on the form and content of his images, but on the political processes that brought them to be.

Not Interesting Enough

Contrary to the spectacular presence embodied in New Deal imagery—documentary, nationalistic, or otherwise—*America*

Recovered presents the stimulus program with a distance and instability that questions the affective presence of federally funded works and the visibility of government institutions. As a collection, the photographs allude to the many distinct shifts that have defined American life throughout the twentieth and now twenty-first centuries. Compared to the New Deal era archive, Ress's *America Recovered* images elicit nearly a century of American global domination, insatiable neoliberal expansion, Bill Clinton's end of "welfare as we know it," racial inequality, gender inequality, income inequality, and the seemingly intractable disconnect between the federal government and the people it ostensibly represents.

With the displacement of governance to the private market and the shrinking social safety net that has come to dominate American politics and budgetary discourses the visual vocabulary used to describe previous stimulus programs and public works projects would be incapable of re-creating the mythic story of the welfare state in action. The insufficiency of photography in this respect is not due to the medium's weakness in performing a similar documentary intent, but because the myth of the liberal state has collapsed. And without new, or updated, forms of aesthetic production, the task of making visible the effect of government policy on the space of daily life remains abstract and unseen. The language of aesthetic critique is still dominated by definitions offered by Burke and Kant. Yet the sublime—infrastructural or otherwise—or the beautiful, cannot capture the aesthetic practices of contemporary governance—or the artistic practices used to critique it—because, as Sianne Ngai describes, the aesthetic features or characteristics of such works, and their media representations are not bound in any systematic way to the affective experiences they evoke.[22] The Hoover Dam itself and the photographs depicting it may produce a sublime experience, but it's unlikely that waiting in a newly installed bus stop will do the same.

Ngai's distinction between form and experience (or knowledge and perception, as she puts it) is only amplified when applied to publicly funded architecture and infrastructure spaces. The aesthetic quality of any single project—and certainly the myriad aesthetics of the project as a whole—is unbound from any cohesive or coherent affective experience.[23] What exactly is the affective experience of a concrete drainage culvert? This disconnect between known aesthetic features and affective experience gives way to Ngai's theory of "interesting" as its own, terminal aesthetic judgment—one that can operate, like the sublime and the beautiful, without any pre-defined concept or content, allowing us to "negotiate the relationship between the possible and the actual," with a distinctly future-oriented temporality.[24] This temporality, in contrast to the sublime, allows the work to linger in the mind, calling the viewer to return, and inserting the image or experience into discursive practice. The interesting begs the question, "why is it interesting?" re-representing the object, work, or experience in order to circulate as a discursive object without temporal constraints.[25] The interesting, according to Ngai, is an aesthetic judgment that can bridge, without solving, the aesthetic-affective unbinding, and one that often relies on external conditions—seriality, data, and other outside referents—to complete both the aesthetic practice and experience of the work in question. The interesting provides a critical framework to analyze Ress's *America Recovered* project against the historical context of landscape photography, text-image artistic traditions, and seriality as a conceptual artistic practice. It also opens a space to critique the stimulus bill as a policy proposal that entailed certain aesthetic and material practices without distinctly claiming them as such.

The strategies of visibility—or the methods of forcing the bureaucratic space of landscape, infrastructure, and building construction and maintenance into the realm of political debate—used by Ress is both an artistic and political practice tied to the production of making stimulus projects both visible and interesting. Many of the images capture a certain environmental vastness, one that verges on emptiness. Others are tightly cropped and documentary. Likewise, the scale and composition of images varies according to subject. But through the repetition of the referent and image relation-ship (as opposed to a repetition of image content), Ress relies on the unedited administrative dataset to make interesting his compilation of photographic evidence. This appeal to outside information is what Ngai calls an "appeal to extra-aesthetic judgments."[26] Systems of bureaucratic data management are certain extra-aesthetic judgements, but so too are political positions and ideologies that code the images within a certain political frame. In linking the image to its stimulus function by captioning it with website information, it is not just the collection of photographs that is rendered aesthetically inter-esting, but the bureaucratic functioning of the state.[27]

If an aesthetic critique of the images veers towards the interesting, their formal composition alludes to the documen-tary passivity made famous in the landmark *New Topographics: Photographs of a Man-altered Landscape* exhibition. *New Topographics* opened in 1975 at the George Eastman House and was described by critic Toby Jurovics as "arguably the greatest show never seen." The collection of photographers and images curated by William Jenkins served to reorient both the field of landscape photography and what the viewer should

expect from images of the American landscape.[28] Writing in the exhibition catalog commemorating the show's re-hanging in 2009, Britt Salvesen notes that the photographs "survey the here and now" without necessarily defining what that means.[29] Salvesen goes on to list a series of subjects captured in many of the photos—street scenes, motorways, parking lots, office parks, "plainly prosaic views"—and says that even today, "the works offer a cool resistance." No doubt scenes and comments that could be uttered upon reviewing Ress's present collection.

The cool resistance Salvesen references has often been interpreted as a unifying style that organized the exhibiting photographers. Indeed, style is one of the aesthetic preoccu-pations surrounding *New Topographics* and what has later been called the "new topographic outlook," defined by curator John Rohrbach as "directness, emotional remove, and attentiveness to humanity's shaping the land." In particular, human inter-vention is not just understood as suburban sprawl, infrastruc-tural development, highway planning, etc., but as a shift from the industrial capitalism that defined the World War II era to a service economy and the alienation brought about by highly repetitive landscapes, corporatization, financialization, and the placelessness that dominates post-war suburban expansion.[30]

Acutely aware that visitors, critics, and historians will no doubt read a cohesive and curated style among the exhibi-tion's artists, Jenkins begins his introduction to the original exhibition catalog by admitting that style is an important problem for the show to contend with. And yet he warns that each individual photograph holds far more meaning; they can't be reduced to simple aesthetic tropes. Jenkins describes the aesthetic underpinnings he used to select the group of photog-raphers through the language of Frank Gohlke, one of the exhibition's artists. Gohlke described his framing and shooting technique as the "passive frame." "Rather than the picture having been created by the frame, there is a sense of the frame having been laid on an existing scene without interpreting it very much."[31]

This idea would seemingly remove any boundaries restricting subject or content driven narratives and give added deference to the photograph's experiential qualities. Gohlke himself captured this best, with a body of work exhibited in the show that didn't adhere to any dominant subject. Gohlke's black and white images captured suburban residential neighborhoods, the open fields of Nebraska, water infrastructure, non-descript industrial buildings, a K-Mart parking lot, and scenes from downtown Los Angeles. Salvesen claims Gohlke's images "do no immediately reveal a unifying idea" and yet they present a version of American landscape that is both typical and specific.[32] The images, according to Salveson, capture a general idea of America by depicting a few of its discrete landscapes. This was a common refrain for visitors entering the Eastman House and viewing the exhibition. The catalog reprint opens with a recording taken on December 14, 1975 of two visitors and their reactions to the show. While viewing the photographs on exhibition, one of the visitors says, "At first they are really stark nothing, but then you really look at it and it's just about the way things are. This is interesting, it really is."[33]

"Interesting" was the same conclusion given by Charles Dearies, writing in one of the exhibition's few reviews in *Afterimage*.[34] But as Ngai has articulated, the interesting serves not as a marker of negative criticism or a linguistic method to sidestep aesthetic judgment altogether, but as an aesthetic judgment in and of itself. For Ngai the interesting is a judgment that embodies both novelty and seriality; one

that attempts to reconcile the rational and the abstract. The interesting reaches far beyond traditional aesthetic boundaries, addressing aesthetic exerpiences that are low in affect and easy to miss.[35] Both Ngai and Jenkins locate the artwork of Ed Ruscha as a type of primordial subject for their respective projects. For Jenkins, Ruscha's work "possessed at once the qualities of rigorous purity, deadpan humor and causal disregard for the importance of the images."[36]

But where Jenkins is occupied with what he sees as the stylistic neutrality of Ruscha's work, Ngai's focus is in its seriality, and in the intertextual possibilities produced by vacillating between the individual and the serial. Part of what makes seriality so important for Ngai is that it imports nonaesthetic qualities, such as external information and conceptual framing, into the realm of aesthetic experience. The serial speaks to a higher order of contextual principles to which the works of art relate. The judgment of interesting alludes to these external, "extra-aesthetic" characteristics that deeply influence our affective and intellectual understandings of the work.

Ress's *American Recovered* fits within this lineage given its aestheticized, detached or neutral stance, and due to the fact that Ress's subjects can only be fully located external to the frame of the image. For Ngai, the notion of type is highly significant for the interesting. The formal breadth of Ress's images questions the intended typological reference—and even the need for such ordering. What exactly is the typology of government funding? Ress answers that question with a broad set of responses, none of which may do much to establish a standard ideal or typological norm. In one image, we see a backhoe moving large boulders in what looks like a grassy riverbed. In another, San Francisco's Golden Gate Bridge is seen in the distance with a building in the foreground and an array of solar panels atop its roof. Only through the caption are we to understand that the subject is the solar panels, paid for by $118,298.00 of stimulus funds. It is left to the viewer to judge the financial merits of any given project. Another image depicts what looks like the interior of a military building with a single, fatigue-clad soldier walking down the hall and away from the viewer. And yet another is a series showing a half-destroyed, wood-framed residential building with a couple of hardhat and construction vest-wearing workers observing from the side. The next image is the same home, now completely destroyed; reduced to a mound of building detritus. Ress's images are both interior and exterior, populated and empty, shifting in frame from perpendicular to angled. Most are taken at ground level, but some are shot from above, and a few from below. Like Gohlke's collection, they offer an *idea* of America, although what that idea is, and what it is trying to represent remains vague and undefined, only somewhat gleaned through the relations established between the images and their textual captions.

Ress's range of employed photographic conventions and each image's stylistic restraint serves to dislodge the subject from any immediate photographic type. In Ngai's reading, this opens a gap between knowledge and perception, prompting the viewer to look elsewhere in order to complete the experience of viewing the whole work. Crucial, then, to Ress's collection of photographs are the adjoining captions he took directly from the Recovery.org website. The captions serve as a typological benchmark linking the images together, forming a bridge between the textual demarcation of subject and the varying affective experiences of viewing. Hence, the aesthetic differences between images matter less than the relationship established *across* the series. These relationships

work to further reinforce Ress's conceptual field by creating myriad affective experiences of both image making and being present in the landscape while also linking these experiences to the viewer's subjective status within the bureaucratic state. The serial, database-driven nature of the stimulus project's management, the seemingly endless material variety of their reality, and—crucially—their near invisibility within the landscape emerge, quietly but coherently, in this way. The captions are important not as simple descriptors associated with the image, but as an aesthetic typology of the state. The cool, bureaucratic, and referent-less dataset becomes the baseline typological form of stimulus funding and thus the state as a material actor in the American landscape. The photographic images of disparate and formally distinct instantiations of that typological referent can only be described as "interesting" instances of the larger political-bureaucratic process.

Based solely on their formal or stylistic language, many *America Recovered* images could easily have been included in the *New Topographics* exhibition. For instance, "City of East Lansing, Michigan" initially appears to utilize the tropes of distance and neutrality celebrated by Jenkins and questioned by later writers. Yet when read, literally as it were, with its caption, the formal and conceptual focus of the image is immediately reoriented and the cognitive/aesthetic divide is shifted from a tableau of empty road and trees to the road as an alley-way paid for by government funds to provide services to a new, market and low-income housing project. The image no longer shows a scene from a town in Michigan, but the pervasive nature of government-financed transportation infrastructure. Without the external, textual reference, the visibility of something as omnipresent as the nation state would remain invisible within this particular scene *and* its photographic representation. It is similarly unlikely the role of the stimulus as alleyway maker has been made visible to the residents of this block.

By reading the images of this book together, *America Recovered* makes a profound claim: that the nation state as a spatial mediator is not visible in the everyday imagination of the citizen and subject population. If anything is meant to follow from this claim, it is not to reify the government, or to reinvest in the mythologizing of New Deal era photography, but to signal the importance of visibility, the promise of discourse, and their constitutive role in representative democracy. By repeating the text-image form *America Recovered* thrusts the landscapes of infrastructural and spatial maintenance into the political realm, making them visible as manifestations of the bureaucratic state *and* as potential for political action.

Ress's ease in shifting between and beyond certain stylistic genres and his desire to mediate the images with textual descriptions makes the project difficult to comprehend or critique on the basis of individual images alone. Ress is inserting a type of visibility into the aesthetic field, inviting viewers to look at his images and see the state at work. More directly, Ress is making a claim that the state itself is invisible, that it works in ways that have become so pervasive that the visual languages of style and form do little to capture its hegemonic presence—whether funding home demolitions in Detroit, Michigan or water infrastructure improvements in Chino, California.

The status of *America Recovered* as a recuperative political project in some sense relies on the discursive power of interest generated through the aesthetic experience of relating images to captions. The collection of images relies not on a sublime judgment to generate a socially constructed experience but for the project to generate enough interest to cue extra-aesthetic judgments in the service of political action. Through Ress's images, the failure of the stimulus bill to make itself visible and interesting cannot solely be blamed on hyper-partisanship or a lack of large-scale, spectacular infrastructure, but that the projects failed to be received as a unified collection of individual projects representing the full scale of the state at work. The collection of projects, extensive as they might have been, failed to be noticed as a broadly constituted infrastructural or economic stimulus; they were, quite often and often quite literally, invisible. This invisibility meant they failed to make any aesthetic claims and therefore any aesthetic impact, either through their material reality or as images transmitted across the media. Without a project of making visible the serial and highly nuanced nature of the state at work, and the multiple expressions state actions take, the Recovery Act projects might simply be relegated as not interesting enough.

Taking Stock:
Chad Ress's Photographs
of the Recovery Act

Miriam Paeslack

Considering Chad Ress's photographs of sites affected by the American Recovery and Reinvestment Act (ARRA), one is struck by contrasting observations: the unassuming neutrality of these images on the one hand, and their potentially provocative political implications on the other. Between the two, Ress's position is not immediately apparent. Does he, as he claims himself, successfully "avoid" revealing his own ideological stance or does his visual language rather present a commentary on this embattled government? Is Ress a critic or an accomplice in ARRA efforts? And how does his own project relate to his hope for proper communication about ARRA policy through stock photography? In a text for *TIME* magazine, Ress explains that he had found different types of data on the government website that documented ARRA projects. In some cases, images were crowdsourced and what "appears to be stock imagery." He speculates whether representing ARRA projects this way "ultimately result[s] in a more accurate, transparent, or historical document" that will be "up to the task of remembering this very important policy."[1] This essay attempts to situate Ress's photographs both as part of a large endeavor of "taking stock" of government measures and the tradition of surveying and organizing visual data in large sets of images; it also situates Ress's work as part of a complex history of photography in dialog with artistic and documentary practices.

The following description of the relation between a photograph's referent and a viewer's options for its further interpretation by the photographer Jeff Wall provides a point of departure for thinking through this issue based on a consideration of the "still" photographic image as an astonishingly nimble medium:

The still picture is the most free visual form, it invites the most free experience. Since it shows only an isolated moment, it cannot and must not show other moments, it can only suggest them. We take the suggestion, and elaborate it ourselves, freely, or very freely, according to who each viewer is, or wishes to be.[2]

Wall's observation suggests the collaborative production of meaning between the photographer, the viewer and the moment. The "still picture" relies on interpretation in order to uncover its entire range of meanings. This is particularly true for Ress's images of recovery projects. They seem to express and combine a number of different agendas. One aims directly at representing the matter-of-fact descriptive text of the projects provided by recovery.gov; the other follows a more interpretive path. Together these approaches, and the fact that they are deliberately left undistinguished, complicates Ress's work. It aligns it with both creative and conceptual modes of representation. This multiplicity of approaches figures directly into the images' form, which appears both documentary, striving to represent accurately and objectively, and fictional, "elaborating" on the subject matter.

Ress himself describes his intentions in a way that supports both the generative side of photography and its use to create an archive of knowledge. He explains that he considers many parameters including "perceived aesthetic opportunity," his initial response to the content of the language, and his desire to create a "representative sampling of the broader stimulus efforts."[3] His photographs challenge their viewers by highlighting a space of interpretive uncertainty. The image remains suspended—undecided—and unfolds meaning that is particularly open to different interpretations.

In his observations about the process of seeing photographs, the American philosopher Kendall Walton touches on this issue:

We have now uncovered a major source of the confusion which infects writings about photography and film: failure to recognize and distinguish clearly between the special kind of seeing which actually occurs and the ordinary kind of seeing which only fictionally takes place, between a viewer's really seeing something through a photograph and his fictionally seeing something directly. A vague awareness of both, stirred together in a witches' cauldron, could conceivably tempt one toward the absurdity that the viewer is really in the presence of the object.[4]

For Walton, fictionalization happens in the process of seeing. "Fictional seeing" suggests seeing the actual thing in the photographs while one really only sees a representation.[5] Walton finds that fiction happens in the process of seeing an image—the photograph "owns" a "remarkable ability to put us in perceptual contact with the world," something he calls "photography's transparency" and which he declares the most important justification for speaking of "photographic realism."[6] Transparency and fiction are related to one another when regarding photographs not as autonomous but as activated and rendered meaningful in the process of their being seen, interpreted, and contextualized.

With their straightforward aesthetic, Ress's forty-one color images of ARRA projects sites, objects, and people suggest a reliably "real" plot just as they inspire something fictitious. It is this asynchronism between transparency (the "suggestion" of

making things appear) and fiction (the application of imagination and interpretation) that Jeff Wall hints at when he
talks about photography as the process of "elaborating" on the
suggestions which any given moment provides.

Ress's images correspond with descriptive captions; the
artist adopted the text verbatim from the ARRA website and
used it as instructions for image making. Text and image,
while clearly related and referential, tell two different stories.
Ress, unsurprisingly, decided for their display in this book
that they be clearly separated from one another; one spread
contains the caption, the next the image.[7] This dissociation
between text and image is rendered even more profound
through photographic means. The images' documentary character seems to underwrite ARRA's explicit call for transparency;
while Ress's choice of subject, such as inclusion of people or
the depiction of a site that might have been chosen to correspond most closely to a caption without being able to exactly
identify its location, places these photographs into the realm of
fiction.[8]

The scope of Ress's images is determined by the range
of projects that were financed by the Obama administration's
2009 ARRA stimulus bill. The website, recovery.gov, was set up
as part of ARRA's requirement "to establish and maintain a user-
friendly, public-facing website to foster greater accountability
and transparency in the use of covered funds."[9] To this end the
administration established recovery.gov as a resource by which
the public might track expenditures. Ress used the same tool
as starting point for conceptualizing his images.[10] Recognizing
this unique opportunity and inspired by "the disconnects—
between text and image—between paying your taxes and how
those funds are spent," Ress used the project descriptions not
only as a guide to ARRA projects, but as a kind of suggestive

script or instruction.[11] These seem to be images, then, that
take into account elements of these descriptions and yet don't
reveal unequivocally what this-or-that measure achieved or
how it was instated. "Elaborating" on these photographs, the
viewer is confronted with multiple meanings.

Part of this polyphony—these layers of pictorial meaning and the tension between transparency and fiction—is
created in the ambiguity of pictorial form as well as in the
space that Ress describes as "disconnects" between text and
image. One way of accessing this space is to take clues from
an artistic practice that routinely relies on textual and visual
means, and that trades languages of description and interpretation: instructional art. This approach originates in the
practice of conceptual artists in the 1960s. Sol LeWitt, an early
proponent of instructional art, famously provided instructions
for artwork such as line drawings, which were to be applied
directly onto gallery or museum walls and which took several
people multiple days to execute.[12] Claiming that, "the idea
becomes a machine that makes the art," LeWitt prioritized
idea, concept, and instruction over its manifestation, and
thus confronted the instructional text with many potential
interpretations.[13] Seemingly transparent, clearly decipherable
instruction renders its artistic execution the subject to interpretation—to fictionalization.[14]

Not surprisingly, others from the Fluxus Movement
in the 1960s and 70s to more contemporary artists such as
Andrea Fraser or Erwin Wurm, have understood instruction
more as a guideline for enactment than for creation. However,
unlike conceptual art, which is concerned with instruction
only insofar as it serves to realize the idea, Ress's work is deeply
committed to both image form and content. In other words,
Ress's work's *content* is based on the website's instruction,

while its form, i.e., its composition and framing are determined by his aesthetic decisions and interpretations.

In this respect Ress's project relates to modernist discussions of photography as a means to capture instantaneously, but also to Jeff Wall's understanding of the still image as suggestive medium. Wall, a photographer who has significantly shaped post-modern theories of photographic representation, is known to use compositional strategies that rely on historic conventions. Both Ress and Wall speak about their subject matter through precise staging. Ress seems to combine different traits of postmodern artistic production: the reliance on rules or signals that submit the creative process to a certain degree of chance and unpredictability as well as the sophisticated determination of an image's content through editorial measures such as framing. Part of this instruction-based creative process resonates with Ress' idea to have captions on their own page, apart from the photo, almost as distinct and independent works of art.

Ress's image of New Hogan Lake presents a somewhat puzzling scenario. As if following a hidden choreography, a hydraulic shovel is distributing large boulders in piles on an open, brown grass-covered plain. The monumental dimensions of the boulders and the diagonal they trace recall ritualistic sites of ancient cultures, only these rocks are clearly being arranged by industrial means. This ambiguity is countered by the image's sophisticated composition. Horizontally divided into two almost perfect halves—of brown earthy bottom and airy blue-white top—the light blue band of a creek and a few dark green bushes on the far right trace the image's dividing horizon line. A clear compositional sensitivity is detectable in the hydraulic shovel's marking of the image's vertical golden ratio on the left; while the clustered boulders trace a diagonal

line connecting the machine's dramatic arm and shovel on the center-left with the picture's foreground, slightly to the right. This image is not a landscape photograph in the classic sense (Ansel Adams comes to mind), nor is it a landscape image in the style of scientific surveys (such as Carleton Watkins's or William Henry Jackson's). Looking for clues and consulting the caption (the instructions), suggests that this is "New Hogan Lake, Valley Springs, California." The task depicted, according to Ress quoting recovery.gov, is to "place boulders in Wrinkle Cove and Whiskey Creek Recreation Areas." It promises "boulders will be used to prevent illegal off-road travel during low lake levels and prevent environmental degradation." The work is being funded through the Recovery Act with $125,000.00.[15]

But what of this instruction has actually figured into this image and what does one's interpretive "elaboration" add to it? This image, as the others in this set, points to Ress's own struggle with the interpretation and systematic organization of the subject of *recovery*. He points out that despite the mandate for transparency, "There are certain aspects of the stimulus bill that seem impossibly opaque to me. I've been limited in the sites I'm allowed to visit and these limitations have become very important. So what you're not seeing here is perhaps as interesting as what you are seeing."[16] Ress's narrative, his fiction, emerges from an interplay between the mundane, descriptive instructions and his attempt at capturing the things that cannot be made visible, by filtering them through the panoramic landscape genre. The work reveals a certain cognitive dissonance between the verbal narrative's plain language and its visual translations' unavoidable transformation of the subject into a highly individual image. Given the same caption, any other artist would produce a different image

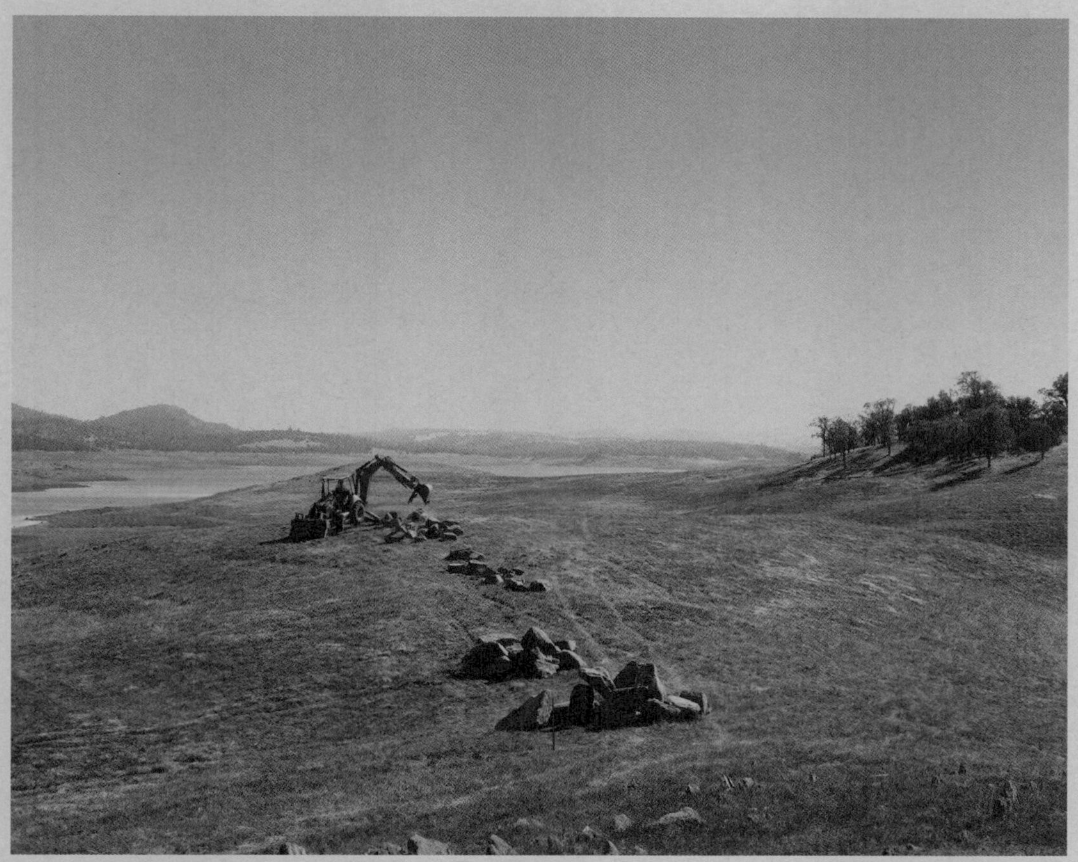

Chad Ress, New Hogan Lake Valley Springs, California, 2009.

and would employ his or her creative imagination in different ways. ARRA's transparency is anything but.

As Bonnie Honig remarks in her foreword, photographic predecessors and influences help put this work into perspective. Roy Stryker, leading protagonist of the Farm Security Administration (FSA), had a documentary vision aimed at representing the overcoming of hardship and of completing public works.[17] FSA photographers, such as Walker Evans and Dorothea Lange, are known to have been instructed by Stryker to create an engaging photographic narrative, to follow a "shooting script," or "a brief but carefully worked out story of what is to be presented."[18] Compared to such a script, for Ress the ARRA captions set a more open agenda, leaving leeway in his determination of the images' form and content. It is not surprising then that Ress takes clues less from Evans and Lange, the two most prominent FSA photographers, but rather from photographers who started their careers during the late 60s and early 70s and who emerged as photographic representation became associated with post-modern questions of authenticity and authorship. Such photographers include Robert Adams, Lewis Baltz, Frank Gohlke, Nicholas Nixon, Stephen Shore, and Bernd and Hilla Becher. They shared an interest in the mundane everyday qualities of American life. Their work was brought to a larger audience's attention with two exhibitions, *Towards a Social Landscape* (1966), and the even more influential *New Topographics* (1975). The latter was organized by William Jenkins who identified a shared concern amongst these predominantly American photographers for the damaging impact of human intervention on the American landscape. The exhibition displayed—in 168 carefully composed, mostly black-and-white prints of streets, warehouses, city centers, and industrial and suburban sites—different interpretations of America's "man-altered landscape." This work carried a political message and reflected, consciously or not, "the growing unease about how the natural landscape was being eroded by industrial development and the spread of cities."[19]

It was during the 1960s and 70s, when the American landscape was receiving such interest, that photography became the medium of choice for *artists* appreciating its particular qualities of speed and suitability to be compared, contrasted and arranged according to typologies of motifs. Jeff Wall's hybrid images, bearing both documentary and fictional characteristics, belong to this category, as do those of Robert Adams, Lewis Baltz, and the Bechers. Wall's large color prints or transparencies (often displayed in light boxes) depict seemingly quotidian yet almost undetectably staged situations. This hybrid work has famously been called "near documentary." It describes pictures that may be reconstructions of events that he witnessed or that may be documentary photographs involving a small degree of intervention by the artist.[20] Such a conflation of observation and creative intervention appears in other artistic scenarios as a result of instructional art or curatorial approaches.[21] What Ress's images share with Wall's and those by his contemporaries is a desire to make transparent what a place looks like while enhancing and amplifying such transparency through the deliberate framing and setting up of a scene. However, transparency, when dramatized, becomes unreal.

In the photograph titled "Rose Creek Bike and Pedestrian Bridge, San Diego, California," Ress places the viewer underneath two broad concrete column–supported highways, which diverge into the frame's left and right upper corners.

Close to the photographer's standpoint in the image's middle ground, a chain link fence cuts horizontally. This composition highlights a sense of the site's inhospitality. The early afternoon sun produces two bold diagonal shadows off both concrete tracks. Cutting through the image plane from the lower left to the upper right these shadows starkly define the photograph's middle ground. Such a high degree of compositional rigor instills a certainty about the image subject, which is revoked once one realizes that the image and its instructions —a "bike/pedestrian bridge to connect with the existing bike path and to provide access cross Rose Creek"—don't seem to match at all. This image does not actually depict the caption's content, but rather a situation that makes the need for such a bridge palpable. The Mike Gotch Memorial Bike and Pedestrian Bridge was actually built in April of 2012 a couple of miles south of the site that Ress photographed. Reports about the opening, which enthusiastically praised its connection of crucial parts of the San Diego bike lane system, made no mention of the fact that its completion was enabled by ARRA. The reports did mention, however, that this project (as is typical for most of those funded by ARRA) had been years in the making but had lacked funding to be completed.[22]

The image's aesthetic and iconography, especially when considered alongside the reports' omission of the funding source, contrast sharply with New Deal image program. Neither the matter-of-fact language of the WPA's survey photography nor the FSA's highly choreographed documentation of the living circumstances of poor farmers and sharecroppers would reasonably have worked if they were as ambiguous as Ress's. The WPA photo surveyor's approach favored depicting unequivocal situations or stages of projects by either presenting people at work, or by showing the work progression, or the completed infrastructural or building project. One of many examples is the WPA-sponsored work for the Golden Gate Bridge in San Francisco.[23] The black-and-white photograph on the following page depicts the construction process of the Lyon Street approach to the bridge.[24] Stemming from a large survey and documentary project, this photograph (and many others like it) brings with it the rich context of systematically assembled and state funded collections, which also distinguishes it from Ress's private initiative.

Another instructional example to discuss formal and content-related decisions in conjunction with the Rose Creek Bridge is Robert Adams's 1974 photo book *The New West*. It was among the first explicit and unapologetic commentaries on American suburbia that had begun to dominate the American landscape since the end of World War II. His photographs of interstate Highway 25 and Mount Vernon Canyon are typically deadpan (see page 37). Highly abstracted and geometrically composed, both photographs capture views onto highways by using the railing separating the street from the surrounding desert landscape as horizontal structuring elements. These photographs' stark, black and white contrasts, together with their square format, condense and amplify the prosaic subject matter with a convincing directness. In his foreword to *The New West*, John Szarkowski described Adams's photographs as "so civilized, temperate, and exact, eschewing hyperbole, theatrical gestures, moral postures, and *espressivo* effects generally, that some viewers might find them dull."[24] However, this seeming lack of theatricality does not preclude Adams's capacity for dramatization, which he achieves through extreme abstraction. Ress's Rose Creek Bike/ Pedestrian Bridge adopts a similar kind of attention to geometry, civility, containment, and aesthetic candor, yet he reintroduces

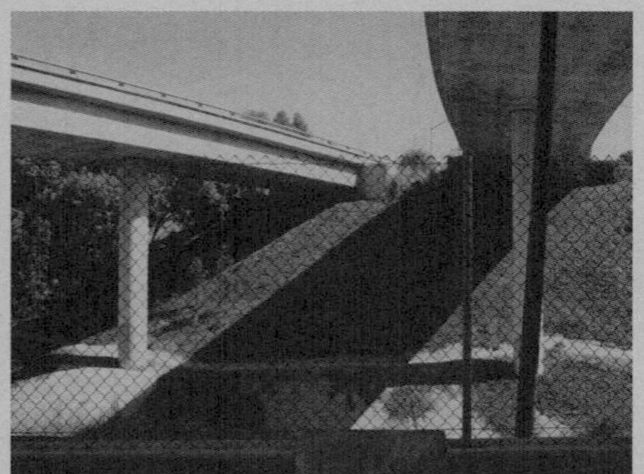

Chad Ress, Rose Creek Bike/Pedestrian Bridge,
San Diego, California, 2009 .

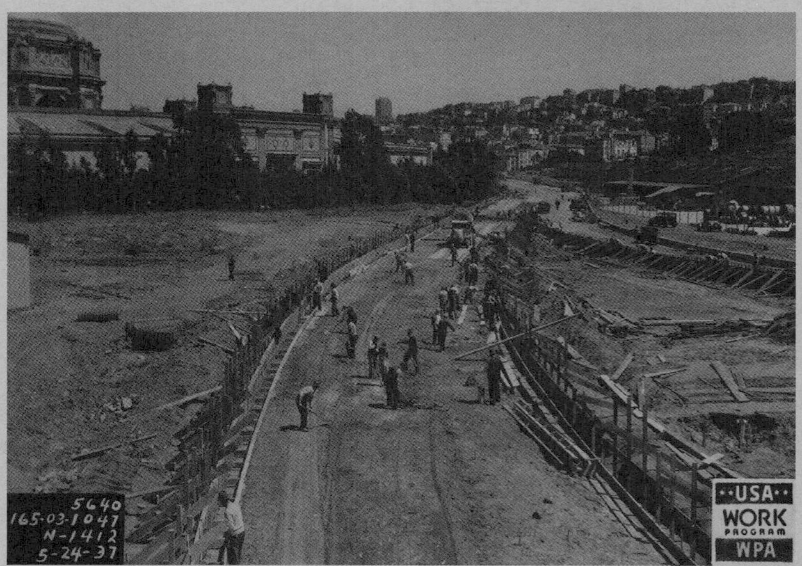

View of WPA crews at work on the Lyon Street approach to the Golden Gate Bridge, May 24,
1937. Photographer unknown, Work Projects Administration, San Francisco, California.

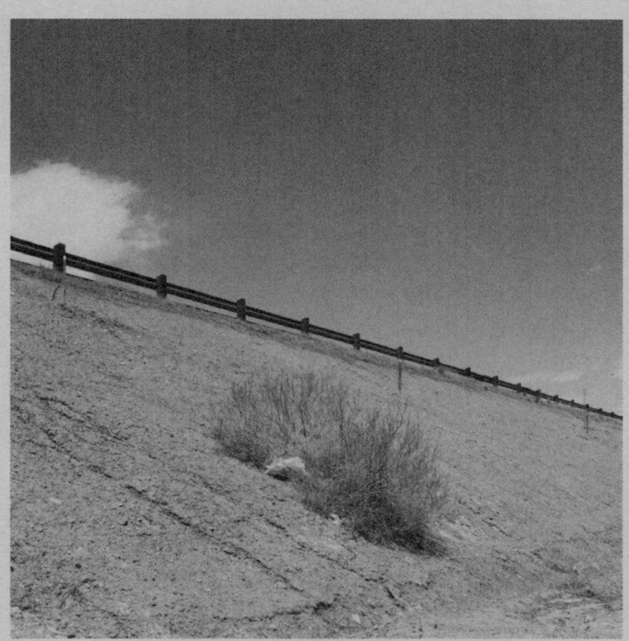

Robert Adams, Along Interstate 25, 1974.

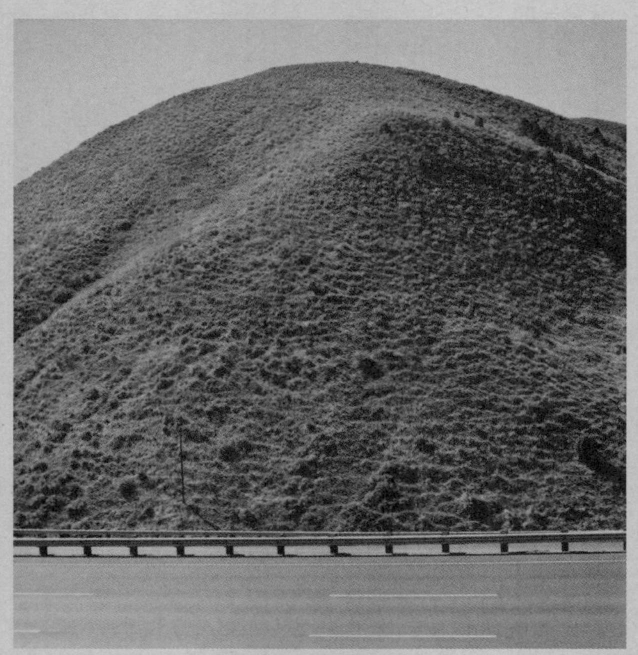

Robert Adams, Mount Vernon Canyon, 1974.

a playful dynamic and narrative of sorts through color, and composition. Jeff Wall, in contrast, working in his mode of documentation went much further to control his image compositions and narrative.[25] Art journalist Arthur Lubow tells the fascinating story of Wall meticulously reconstructing a site in a studio, a "club exterior—the columns and grille-work of the facade, the gum-spotted sidewalk, the concrete curb," when it had turned out that it was too heavily trafficked and therefore not accessible with his large-format camera.[26] Compared to this approach, Ress and Adams appear almost casual and open to happenstance.

The documentary language of Ress's Fullerton Dam image is countered by his compositional choices. Featuring browns and grays, concrete, dry and leafless plants upon a gray sky, its central element is an almost Palladian linear symmetrical concrete structure divided by the vertical dam's tower in two perfect halves. To each side of the tower, concrete enforcements block a stream of debris or boulders from rolling down the hill. A water puddle has formed at the bottom center of the image in front of the tower, collecting all kinds of detritus. A coarse metal grid covers the front length of the tower and makes it look like a part of a fortress. This composition evokes symmetries of Renaissance stage sets. The "instruction" is full of action items such as "construct log boom" or "keep debris from reaching the intake tower," but it distills into an even more abstracted image than that of the bike path in San Diego. The transparency of this project's choreography is rendered opaque through interpretive measures that borrow both from conceptual approaches and a deep knowledge of the language of western art.

Fullerton Dam is part of the Fullerton Reservoir on East Fullerton Creek in Orange County, California. It was built in

1941 for the US Army Corps of Engineers and measures 46 feet high and 575 feet long. While Ress's picture focuses on the dominating architectural structure of the dam tower, it neither gives a sense of the site's dimensions nor of the location for the log boom. The website of Lucille Roybal-Allard, the congresswoman for California's 40th Congressional District, reveals that "the stimulus money" was allotted to fund an array of additional measures beyond a log boom. For example, it was used to remove "graffiti along channels and tributaries of the river, clear non-native vegetation in the soft bottom areas of the river in the Glendale Narrows area, replace and maintain channel fencing along Compton Creek"; and remove "vegetation… on Corps dams."[27] Such additional knowledge reveals Ress's deliberate reductive choice of image subject. It yet again amplifies the cognitive dissonance when trying to align the captions with their images. Considering Ress's reductionism, it is instructive to compare his image of a dam to Margaret Bourke-White's iconic New Deal image of the Fork Peck dam and its history.

Henry Luce of *LIFE* magazine assigned the documentation of the erection of Fort Peck Dam at the Missouri River in Montana to Bourke-White (1904-1971) in 1936. Her most iconic image of that series was called "Fort Peck Dam, Montana," and its cropped version was famously featured on the inaugural cover of *LIFE* magazine in 1936. Here, just like in Ress's image, but unlike the functional and anonymous photo-documentations of the WPA, the motif and its caption don't exactly align. This is not the dam but the dam's spillway and the piers of an unfinished elevated highway. This was located some three miles from the actual dam and was completed four years later in 1940. Bourke-White made savvy use of this colossal concrete structure, which unfolded

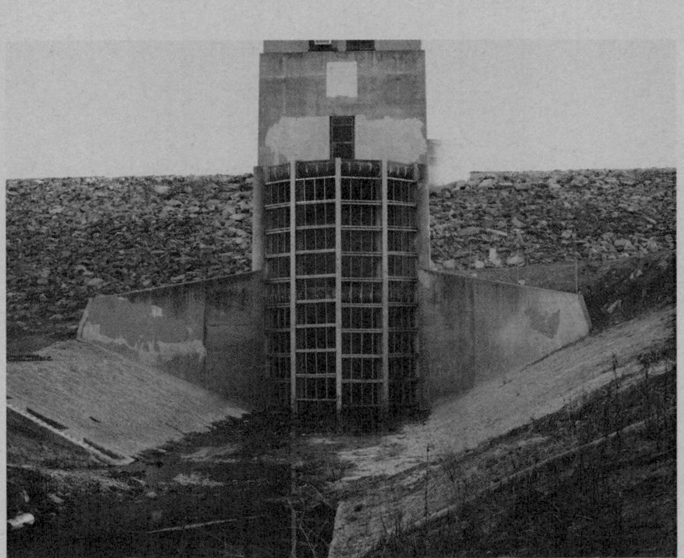

Chad Ress, Fullerton Dam, Fullerton, California, 2009.

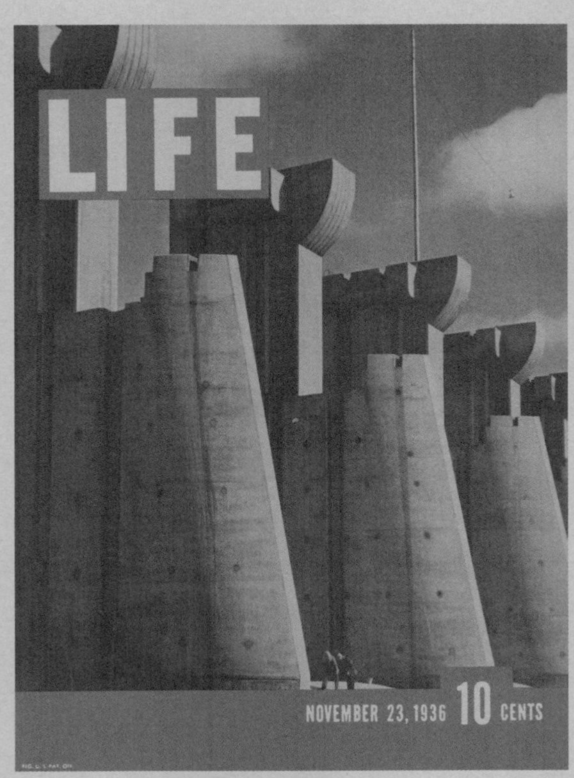

LIFE magazine, issue one, November 23, 1936. Cover photo of the Fort Peck Dam by Margaret Bourke-White.

its dramatic effect most impressively in its incomplete state. Once the highway was built, these floodgates lost their magic semblance to battlements and looked more like any other industrial concrete structure. It is today widely recognized that this image "solidified Fort Peck Dam's status as an icon of the machine age" and that Bourke-White created "a vivid illustration of the power of technology to dwarf humankind."[28] Jordan Carver, in his text in this volume, speaks of an "infrastructural sublime" that links the "vast scale of infrastructural development with the governing power of the state as the only feasible institution that could successfully accomplish such feats." Chad Ress's image of Fullerton Dam, which similarly leaves questions about proportions and work quality unanswered and keeps the project's essential tasks ambiguous, proves a sense for compositional priorities equal to Bourke-White. However, his image doesn't speak of an industrial achievement of aesthetics, technology, and civilization but rather of obsolescence and its corresponding sublime. Examining Ress's image, one starts questioning those very achievements and their significance today.

Bourke-White had been sent out to document this massive building project with the assumption that she would use the camera as a documentary tool. And indeed, her photographs would become what turned out to be the first photo reportage of many published by *LIFE*. This episodic and narrative use of photography became the lingua franca of photojournalism and publishing for the next forty years. The black-and-white photographs by Bourke-White's generation of photographers (Robert Capa, Henri Cartier-Bresson, Gerta Taro, and others) formed the public image of wars, famines, and economic development across the globe for viewers in Europe and North America well into the 1970s. Bourke-White's photograph, however, superseded mere documentation. It facilitated most favorable "elaboration" by its mass audience on the subject of New Deal Projects. *LIFE* editors expressed their awe at Bourke-White's approach, pointing out that instead of getting the documentation of a building they got "a human document of American frontier life instead, which, to them at least, was a revelation."[29] Bourke-White's affirmative and humanistic pictorial vocabulary corresponded with a growing hunger to witness events and conflicts as well as the rapid emergence of photojournalism more generally.

Ress's Fullerton Dam, in comparison, speaks a very different language. A kind of post-industrial fatigue sets in, and the erosion of infrastructure in an age of combatted governmental influence becomes apparent. Ress's refusal to show the actual stimulus measure at the Fullerton Dam underlines this intention. His enigmatic photograph alienates its subject, rendering the dam a symbol of slow decay, disrepair, and neglect. Ress seems uninterested in cropping or staging the dam—as a New Deal agenda might have prescribed—but he chooses to omit the achievements of the dam project's retrofitting by visiting the site before any action took place and by obscuring the dam tower's activity and function. What we as viewers apprehend is therefore the decline of the sense of "the power of technology to dwarf humankind" instilled by Bourke-White almost eighty years earlier.

While the majority of Ress's images are unpopulated landscapes or cityscapes, he sometimes includes or even foregrounds people in his photographs. This approach is mostly used when ARRA funding is supplied to provide public institutions, such as museums, prisons, libraries, or archives, with salaries for employees or equipment for occupants and users. Sitters are never identified by name and instead appear as signifiers of the impact of funding on people's lives. These are not portraits in the conventional sense but rather images of people supported by ARRA funding or—still—left in perilous social and economic circumstances by the recession. Ress's presentation of human protagonists is never coincidental and often appears overtly staged.

In the image accompanying the caption "Boysville of Michigan," a girl is seated at a small desk facing an empty wall. She is positioned slightly off the image's center to the left. The tidy yet somewhat shabby room's nondescript carpet and turquoise and eggshell–colored wall suggest an institutional setting. The wall is lined, at about one third of its height from the ground, by a brown, wooden band and a horizontal strip of electric outlets. This division's location coincides with the height of the seated girl's head. Her concentrated body language is contrasted by her casual outfit—she wears a white hooded sweatshirt, gray sweatpants, and pink fake-fur slippers. Ress chose to capture her facing the wall, which contradicts the human impulse to assess a room by looking inward. This odd scene triggers more questions than it answers.

Boysville of Michigan was founded in 1948. Initially a boarding school for Catholic boys deemed troubled, this program was built on land previously owned by Henry Ford. In a 2014 article announcing the closing of Boysville's Macon campus, the *Tecumseh Herald* explained that the expansion of children's services for Holy Cross Children's Services [formerly Boysville of Michigan] included a whole array of public service institutions such as "other residential campuses, group homes, charter schools, foster care homes, supervised independent living programs, day treatment, and other services" across the state of Michigan.[30] The girl, Ress's photograph seems to suggest, might then be part of a program for youth that was supposed to benefit from ARRA funding. Perhaps the closing of the Macon campus could have been prevented, or it is the result of a post-ARRA impact consolidation of sites and support for children and youth in need. As in his other images, the scope of the funding measure and its exact location is not addressed. Most likely, it was not known to Ress and, more importantly, was not central to his pursuit. What is made very clear by the captions, however, is the amount of funding the government provided for this initiative.

This is a touching portrait, even if the girl's face is not visible. Seated facing the wall, she appears vulnerable, seen without seeing, seemingly unaware that she's being photographed. The domestic and the public interact somewhat awkwardly here, which adds to a sense that the girl's circumstances are uncertain and temporary. The humanity of this image's motif and the dollar amount of its caption make for an ambiguous pair.

Uncertainty on a collective scale was the subject of Dorothea Lange's documentation of unemployed and impoverished Californians in her work for Roy Stryker's FSA effort. The breadth of her photographic vocabulary ranged from scenes observed on the street, which were probably captured in instantaneous single images, to her famously edited image series. Her published images were the product of careful selection and cropping, such as her well-known "Migrant Mother." Lange's protagonist in a different photograph titled "Man beside a Wheelbarrow" taken in San Francisco in 1934 remains anonymous, just like Ress's girl. His head bent forward, the wheelbarrow next to him turned upside-down, this scene speaks of despair and resignation.

The girl in Ress's photograph joins the chorus of Americans

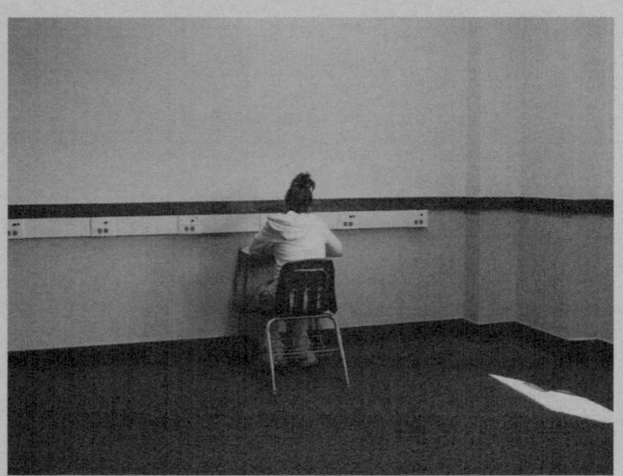

Chad Ress, Boysville Of Michigan, Detroit, Michigan, 2010.

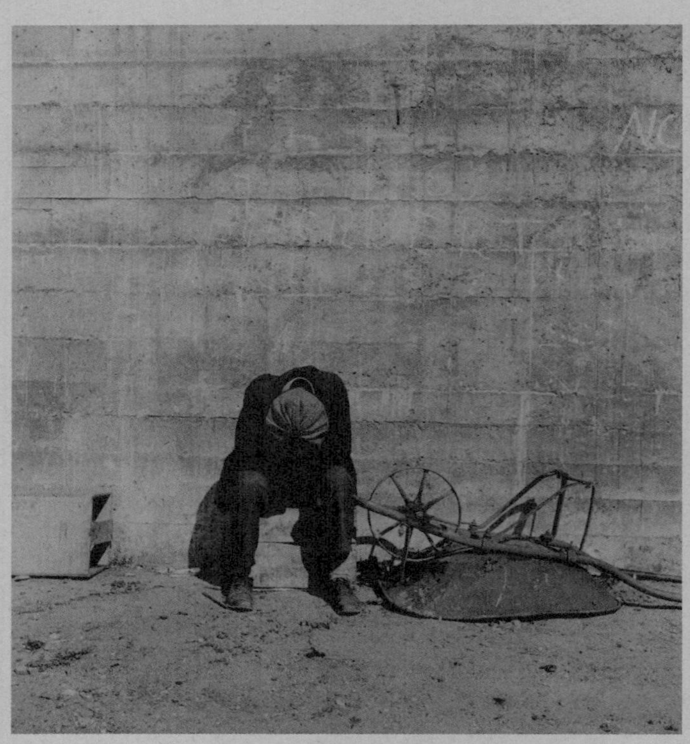

Dorothea Lange, Man Beside Wheelbarrow, 1934.

that have been affected by the recession and that benefit from government measures. While Lange's and Evans's photographs captured the challenging, often devastating circumstances of the Depression, with the understanding of creating an image of a nation in recovery from hardship, Ress's photographs that include people seem more toned down and to avoid generalizing claims about the situation of children and youth in disciplinary institutions, for example. As usual and typical for a post-conceptual artist, he seems to count on the viewer's interpretation and speculation instead of guiding the reading of this image. This lack of resolve is deliberate.

Lange's images can be grouped in two distinct categories: the vast majority are preserved on contact sheets and stored out of sight in archives; a handful of her photographs have come to serve as iconic symbols of despair and resilience. Ress's body of work, even though he stated his aim of creating "a representative sample" of recovery projects, remains much smaller and never aspired to or carried the charge of having been commissioned for such a monumental task.[31]

Another of Ress's images attests to this modesty and aesthetic containment. The photograph of a simple sheet metal shelter shows a metal roofed structure of four posts. Some of the roof's cladding has fallen off. The hut, placed right in the image center, was erected on a sandy shore, which looks like part of an artificial landscape. The elementary quality of this image resonates with the artificiality of the image's subject, the unrealness of earth itself. The band of water in the image's middle ground seems to have gathered as a result of mining or the construction of a dam. According to the ARRA-provided caption, the hut is located in the New Mexican high desert at Cochiti Lake. Cochiti Dam was authorized under the Flood Control Act of 1960, which was further amended in 1964 to

allocate water resources for the development of fish, wildlife, and recreational resources. 62,000,000 cubic meters of water was gathered under this amendment for initial pool fill and sufficient resources were provided to offset annual evaporation losses. Ress's photograph shows a fragment of this recreational area, which appears to have fallen into disrepair.[32] Devoid of people, Ress's scene does not acknowledge the fact that this is a recreational site at all, a place for leisure and enjoyment. Instead it looks like a post-apocalyptic landscape.

The Cochiti Lake image recalls the Bechers' work, in which single images of the same type of building are set up in typological matrices. Always photographed under an overcast sky, the individual structure and its site are rendered flat, shadowless, secondary to the meaning of verisimilitude, repetition, and the potential monotony of industrial reproduction. Ress's primal hut stands on its own but joins another typology, one that tries to match material culture and production with the politics of recovery and financial relief efforts. This formal resemblance of Ress's work to the Bechers's, triggers, yet again associations with two *New Topographics* artists, Robert Adams and Lewis Baltz.

The critic Sean O'Hagan related their work to Walker Evans's for the FSA adding another facet to the way in which we can read Ress's photographs. O'Hagan detected an oblique nod in the *New Topographics* show toward the late work of Walker Evans, who had "photographed the vernacular iconography of American road signs, billboards, motel and shop signs." But while Evans' photographs for today's observer "carry the romantic undertow of an almost vanished America", the *New Topographics* photographs focused on the utterly unromantic [then] here and now. John Szarkowski's observations about *New Topographics* participant Robert Adams's work

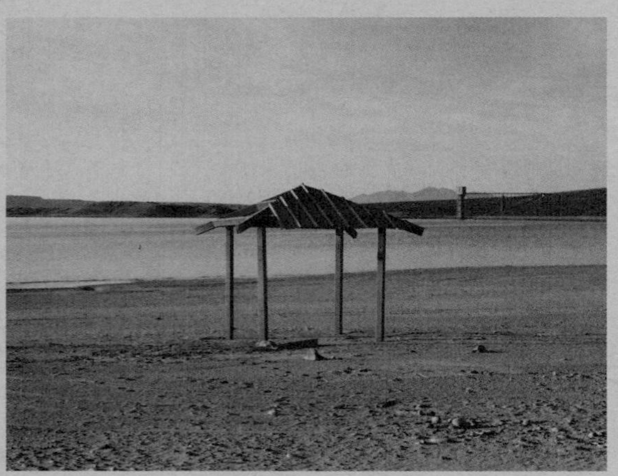

Chad Ress, Cochiti Lake, Albuquerque, New Mexico, 2010.

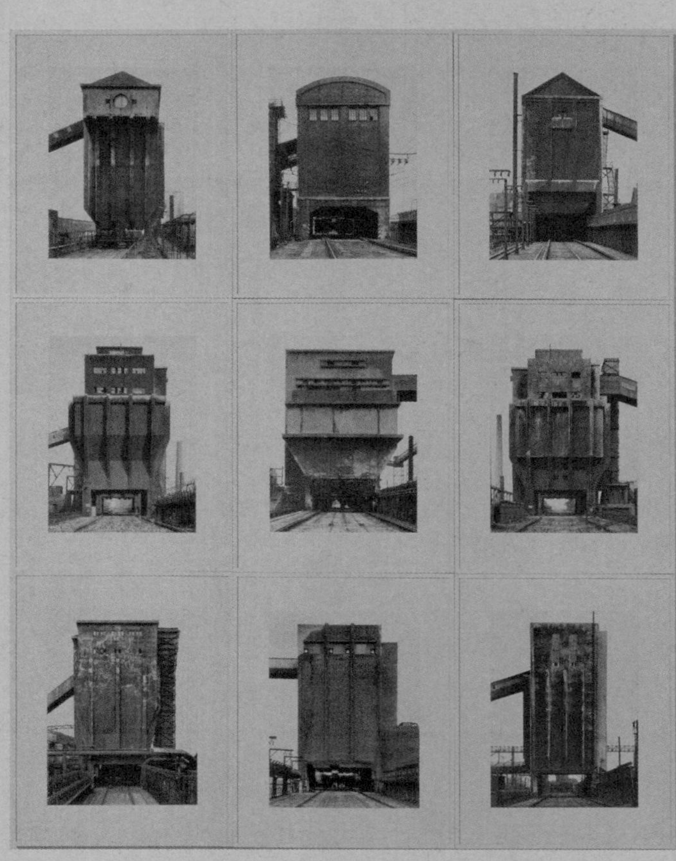

Bernd and Hilla Becher, Coal Bunkers, 1966–1999.

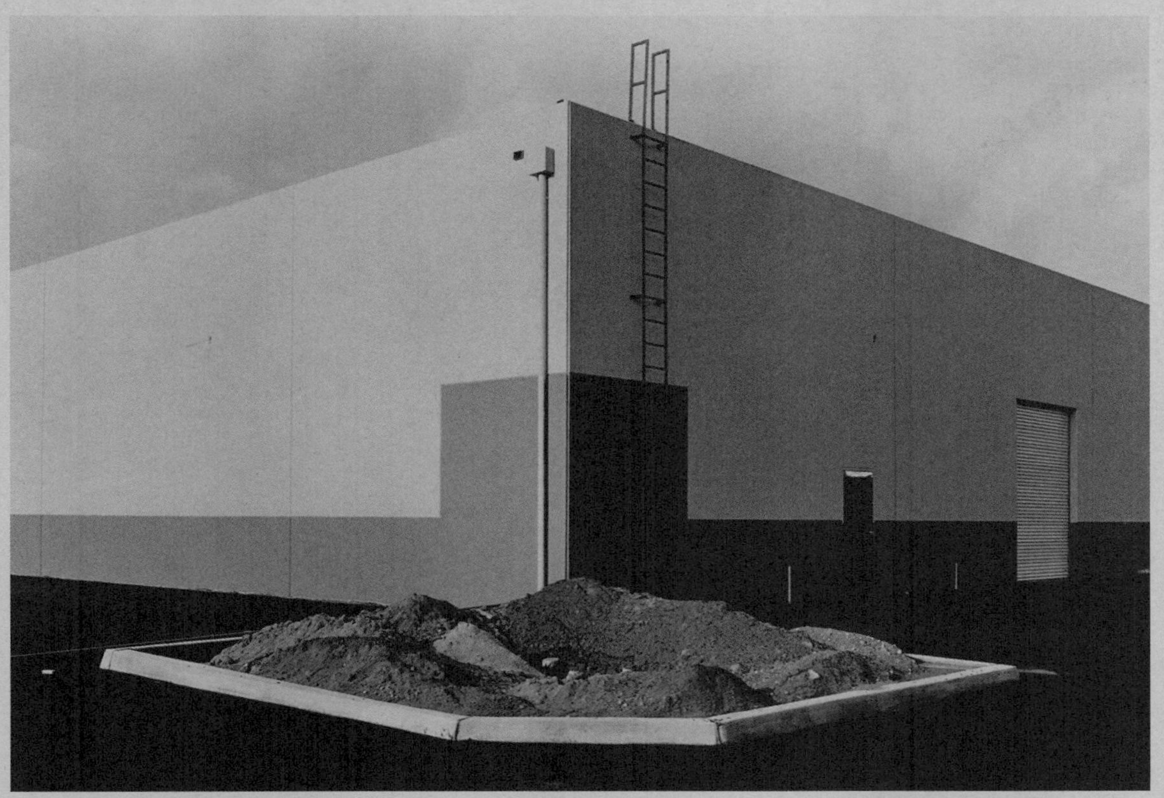

Lewis Baltz, South Corner, Riccar America, 3184 Pullman, Costa Mesa, The New Industrial Parks, near Irvine, California, 1974

summed up this particular understanding when he pointed out that Adams had "discovered in these dumb and artless agglomerations of boring buildings the suggestion of redeeming virtue. He has made them look not beautiful but important, as the relics of an ancient civilization look important. He has even made them look, in an uninspiring way, natural."[33] Similarly, Ress's choice of unassuming subjects and sites that barely seem to even relate to ARRA works render his subject matter important and present it in a way that contradicts a viewer's expectations. By choosing sites of varying elusiveness, he assigns them significance.

Ress navigates the complex field of contemporary photography with an awareness of its rich heritage. While contending with and liberally following the instruction of the information of ARRA provided captions, he admits to second guessing his attempt at disregarding his own ideological bias.[34] He knows that such intention is most likely impossible to achieve. Ress, like Wall or even the nineteenth century photographic explorers of the American West, cannot avoid revealing his own intentions and biases. Ress's intention to create a representative sampling, an overview of ARRA sites suggest his hope for an almost quantifiable, quasi-scientific output. Predecessors of such feats, landscape surveyors were frequent during the second half of the nineteenth century as part of American western expansion. Their achievement was, however, ultimately both measurable by quantity *and* quality. In discussing late nineteenth century landscape photography in the US, Joel Snyder emphasizes the qualitative dimension of such ventures suggesting a formative relationship between the land, its photographic representation, and "the character of photography itself."[35] This relationship both renders the landscape

image political—in the nineteenth as well as the twenty-first century—and confirms photography's adaptability to changing circumstances. It reveals Chad Ress's driving impulses and what defines the tension between transparency and fiction in his work.

Ress's landscapes, interiors, and portraits remind viewers of the current concerning decline in public regard for government intervention in the United States. He achieves this by editorializing the matter-of-fact language of ARRA project descriptions while neither suggesting a coherent narrative as the New Deal photographs often did, nor approaching his subjects with the *New Topographics*' outspoken critique of human-altered environmental conditions. Ress's morale lies in both the drama and the unobtrusiveness of *maintenance*, the often-subtle process of "providing a person with the necessities of life" as Merriam Webster defines it. Picturing the maintenance of infrastructure means to attempt the complex task of visualizing a phenomenon that is both fleeting and mostly unobserved.[36] His photos suggest the perseverance of state-sponsored measures in the face of today's threats at dismantling important government functions altogether. These photographs make palpable the fact that the "complex and contradictory legacy"of the Obama administration cannot be easily deconstructed.[37] This massive recovery effort's sincere attempt at transparency and accountability is affirmed and prepared for posterity through an equally sincere and playfully interpretive depiction.

In conclusion, the wider importance of Ress's photographic depictions and his goal of creating a "representative not exhaustive archive" is most palpable when discussed in the context of large image collections representing ARRA projects—most notably, *crowd sourced* and *stock photography*.[38]

Both generate massive outputs of digital imagery. Both types of mass-generated images provide a framework for understanding how Ress's work walks a line between objectivity and critique.

Initially, the recovery.gov website did not feature photography at all "and instead opted for data visualization technologies such as interactive and searchable data banks."[39] This eventually changed, however, and the site, which has since been taken down, included stories with crowd-sourced images.[40] That meant that the site grew uncurated as it became crowdsourced, as anyone could submit images for consideration. At the same time, the website also began hosting stock imagery: the site hosted the most uncurated and the most curated content together, in both cases giving up control.[41] Megan Garber of *The Atlantic*, talking about stock images, points out that one quality they share "is the 'unique perspective' presented in the composition of the photos themselves." She quotes a shutterstock photographer saying "when shooting a stock photo, you want to think not just about capturing an image, but also about creating a product that will visually pop, particularly against the white backdrop of a web page." It is this photographer who explains to her that "by twisting a photo just a bit… you can create an image that will embody stock's other-worldly appeal."[42] This generic vocabulary and message is no surprise considering that, as Garber points out, "To see a stock image is… to know you're seeing a stock image."[43] Bearing this in mind, the collective image of America's post-2009 economic recovery on recovery.gov started to look like a perfect advertisement for a country presumably on the upswing, glossy, with the sun rising, featuring cute kids and caring doctors. Stock photographs are not only determined by such an agenda but also only function when curated.

Their highly manipulative and highly political nature transpires on both the iconographic and curatorial level. Theirs is the bureaucrat's and politician's corporate language of advertising and branding.

Ress generates a master narrative of maintenance while he bewilders and dazzles his viewer. The languages of stock photography, however, conveys a visual message without a specific audience in mind and suited to an unknown deployment. Stock images are therefore without room for interpretation or

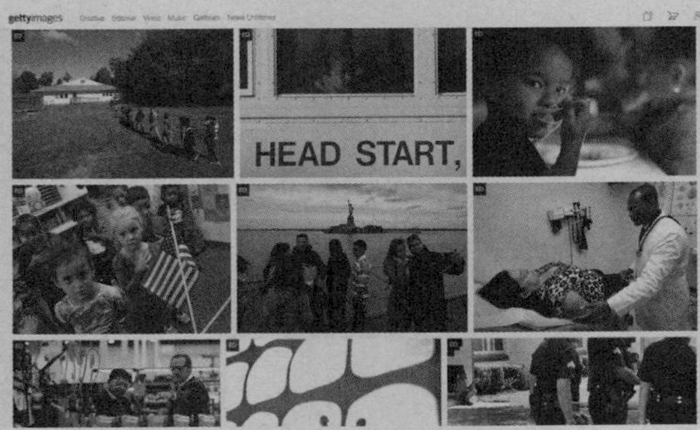

Recovery Act stock photographs, Getty Images.

contestation. Different from stock photo work, Ress deliberately leaves questions unanswered. His work challenges the ownership of this archive of images created of ARRA projects.[44] Given that there is no consolidated or systematically managed repository suggests that, unlike the publicly owned image archive of FSA imagery, the mental and ideological place of government-supported recovery today resides in the embattled zone of the internet. To call stock photographs "owned by the public" is simply enabling the government's further withdrawal from funding cultural efforts. Chad Ress's work and his controlled and creative employment of photography is therefore of particular importance. His effort to complicate and render oblique government measures in the aftermath of the Great Recession should be an alert to the dangerous suggestion that stock-photos and their highly reductive message might be suitable replacements for a contextualizing and critical depiction. Ress's work reminds us of the crucial importance and evolving task of maintaining and training our visual literacy in order to enable deep readings of images.

Ress's work has to be understood as part of the historical lineage of landscape photography, which has always juggled the quest for documentary representation and systematization on the one hand and photography's enormous suggestive, interpretive and manipulative capacities on the other. Transparency, while the declared aim of any photographic surveyor, never operates on its own. The democratic quest for transparency and comprehensiveness is always joined by its interpreting and reflecting partner, fiction. Artists like Ress, Wall, Adams, Baltz and the Bechers, each in their own way, have used this relationship on behalf of their creative endeavors and have kept challenging and provoking reactions and responses. Ress's unique challenge amongst these artists is his place in a generation obliged to take a stance, in the age of mass distributed digital imagery. He lives in an era that promotes "un-creative" artistic production that suggests deliberate use, appropriation, and reuse of parts of original works of art.[45] His own fascination with stock photography on the one hand, and his clear embrace and appropriation of predecessors' aesthetic strategies on the other, both typify contested positions between which Ress and artists of his moment find themselves. His artistic language and use of the medium might be understood as a photographic metalanguage that engages photography's enormous technical and compositional capabilities assessing the balance between the documentary and fictional each time anew.

America Recovered

Chad Ress

Long Beach Opera
Long Beach, California

National Endowment for the Arts Grant to support the
preservation of jobs that are threatened by declines in
philanthropic and other support during the current
economic downturn.

Amount funded by Recovery Act: $50,000.00

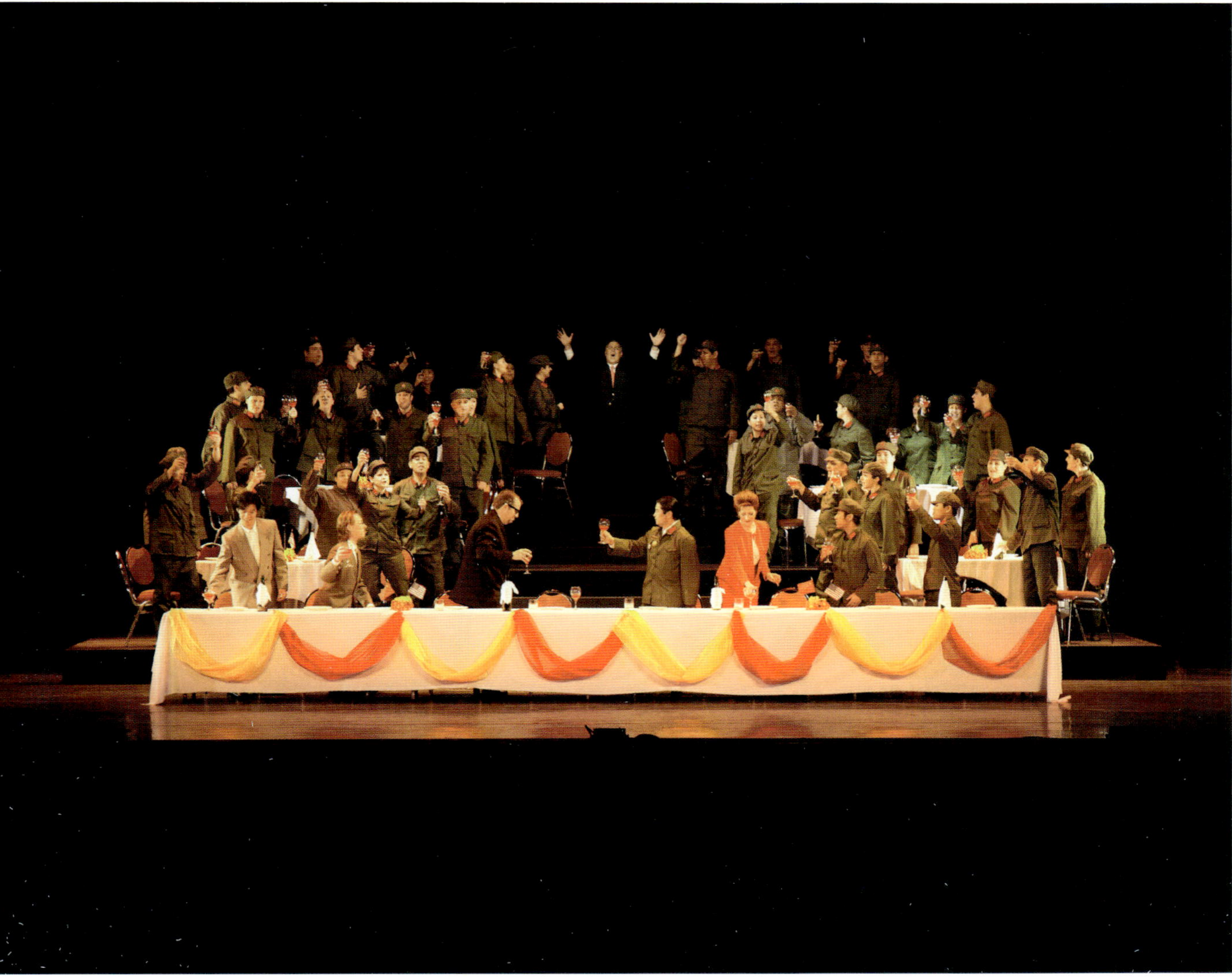

Conservation Corps
Goleta, California

Project work consists of using chainsaws and hand tools to cut remaining vegetation. All vegetative material laying on the forest floor will be picked up and stacked in piles for future burning.

Amount funded by Recovery Act: $50,000.00

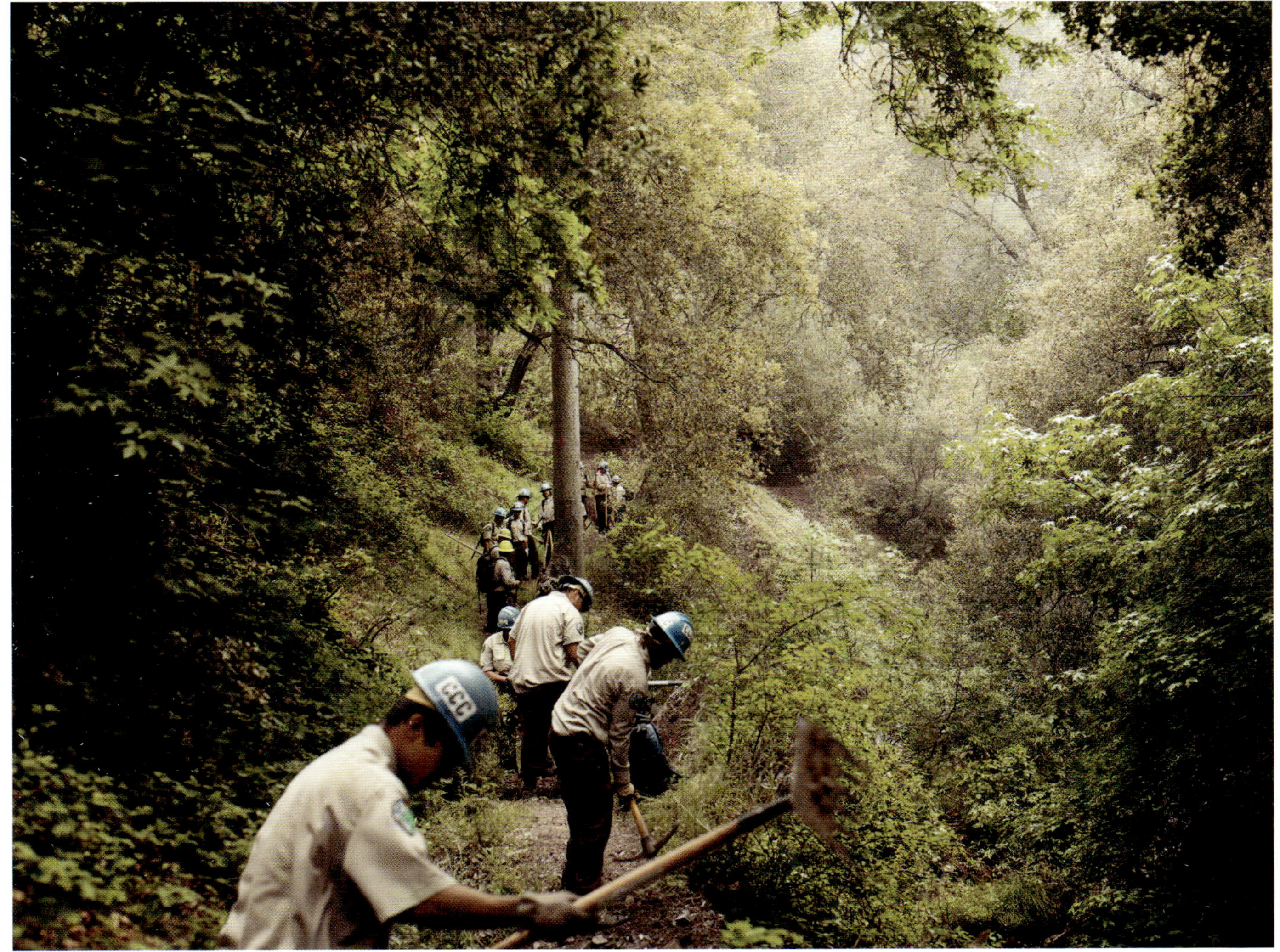

New Hogan Lake
Valley Springs, California

Place boulders in Wrinkle Cove and Whiskey Creek Recreation
Areas. Boulders will be used to prevent illegal off-road travel
during low lake levels and prevent environmental degradation.

Amount funded by Recovery Act: $125,000.00

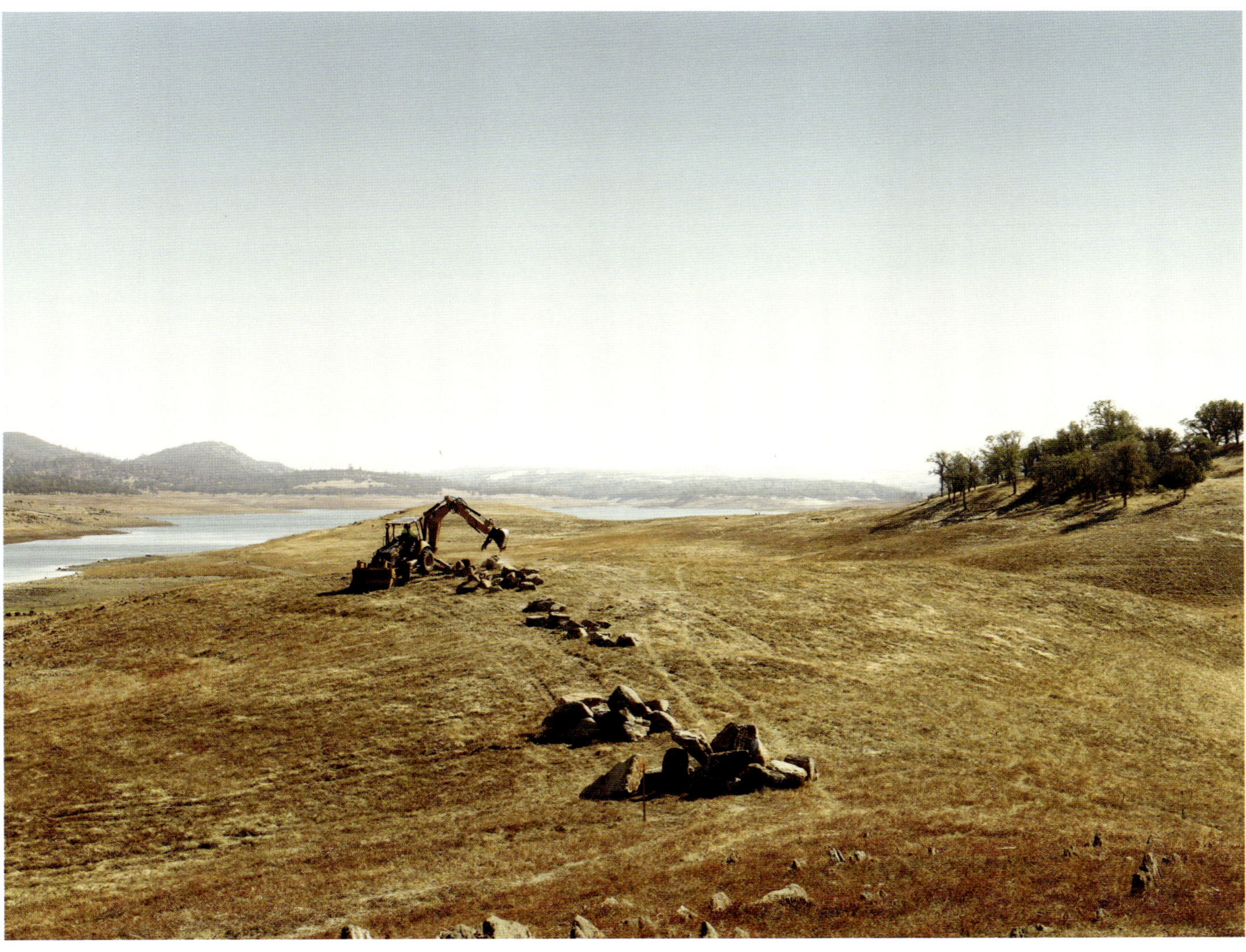

Seeds, Sleeping Bear Dunes
Empire, Michigan

Northwest Michigan Youth Conservation Corps will work with park personnel to repair 15 miles of deteriorating hiking trails at Sleeping Bear Dunes National Lakeshore. Trails will be brushed, tread surfaces repaired, and erosion control devices cleaned, repaired, and installed. Signs will be repaired or replaced and trail markers will be installed.

Amount funded by Recovery Act: $50,000.00

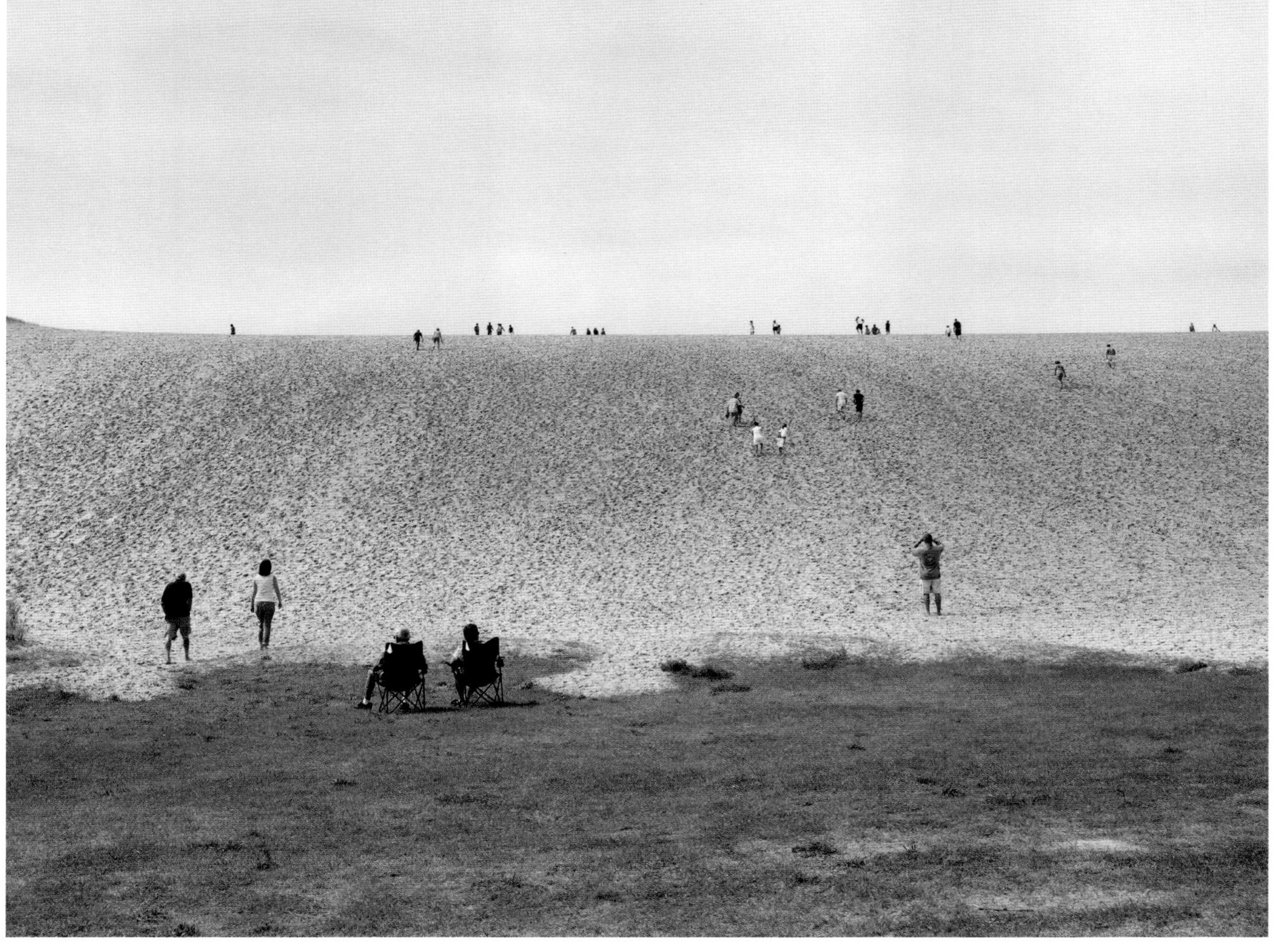

Golden Gate National Recreation Area
San Francisco, California

Grant for an assesment of the environmental impact of installing
an underwater transmission cable in the San Francisco Bay
and photovoltaic panels on Alcatraz Island to end the island's
reliance on diesel generators.

Amount funded by Recovery Act: $118,298.00

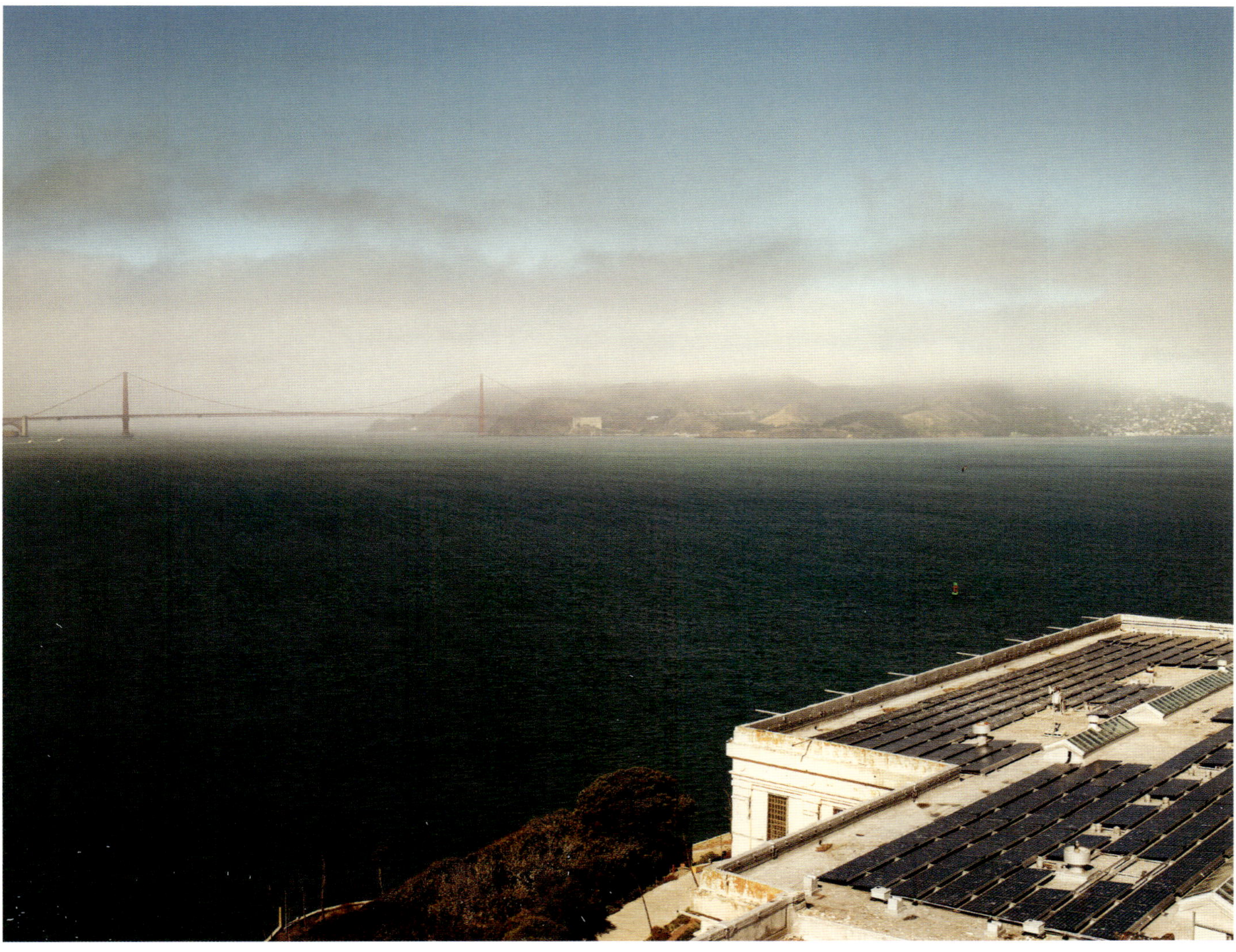

Magnolia Marsh Restoration
Huntington Beach, California

Huntington Beach Wetlands Conservancy—a 41-acre site
that will be restored into a vital wetlands by bringing in tidal
flow, buiding up levees, and replanting native plants.

Amount funded by Recovery Act: $3,200,000.00

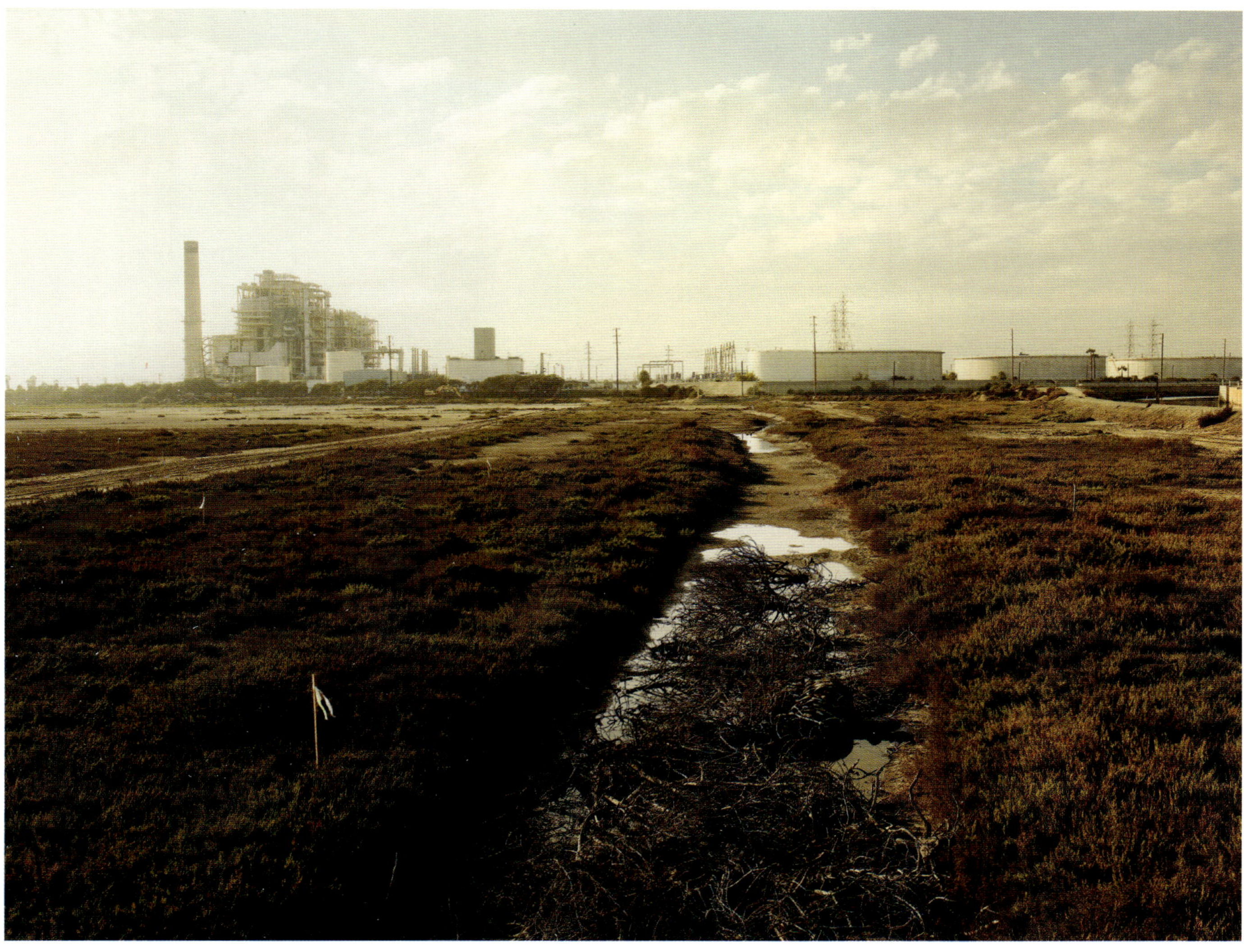

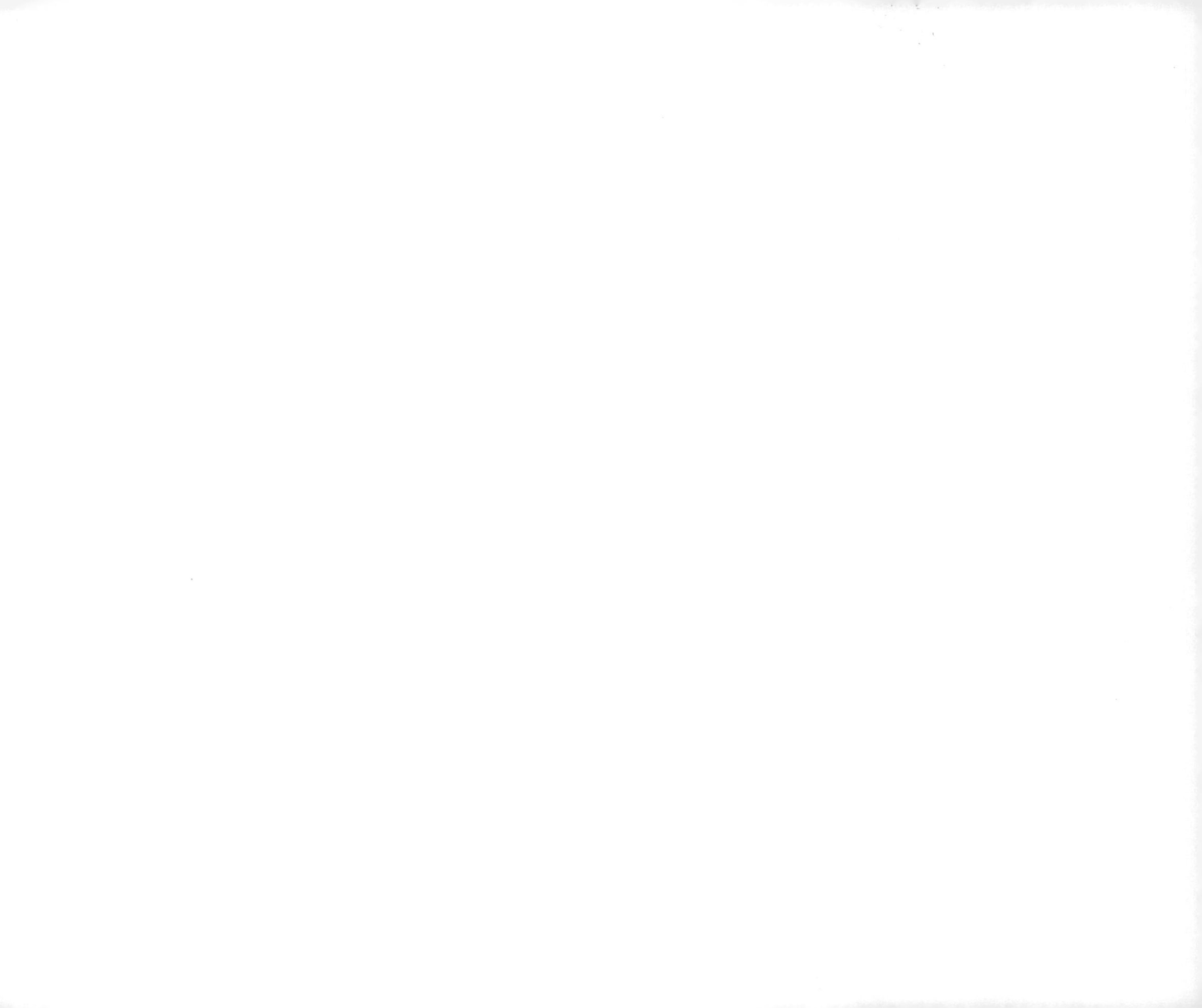

Brownfields
Lincoln Park, Michigan

The City plans to use the grant to develop an inventory of Brownfields within the Community, and then perform environmental assessments on priority sites to identify issues of concern and help prepare them for sale and/or redevelopment.

Amout funded by Recovery Act: $200,000.00

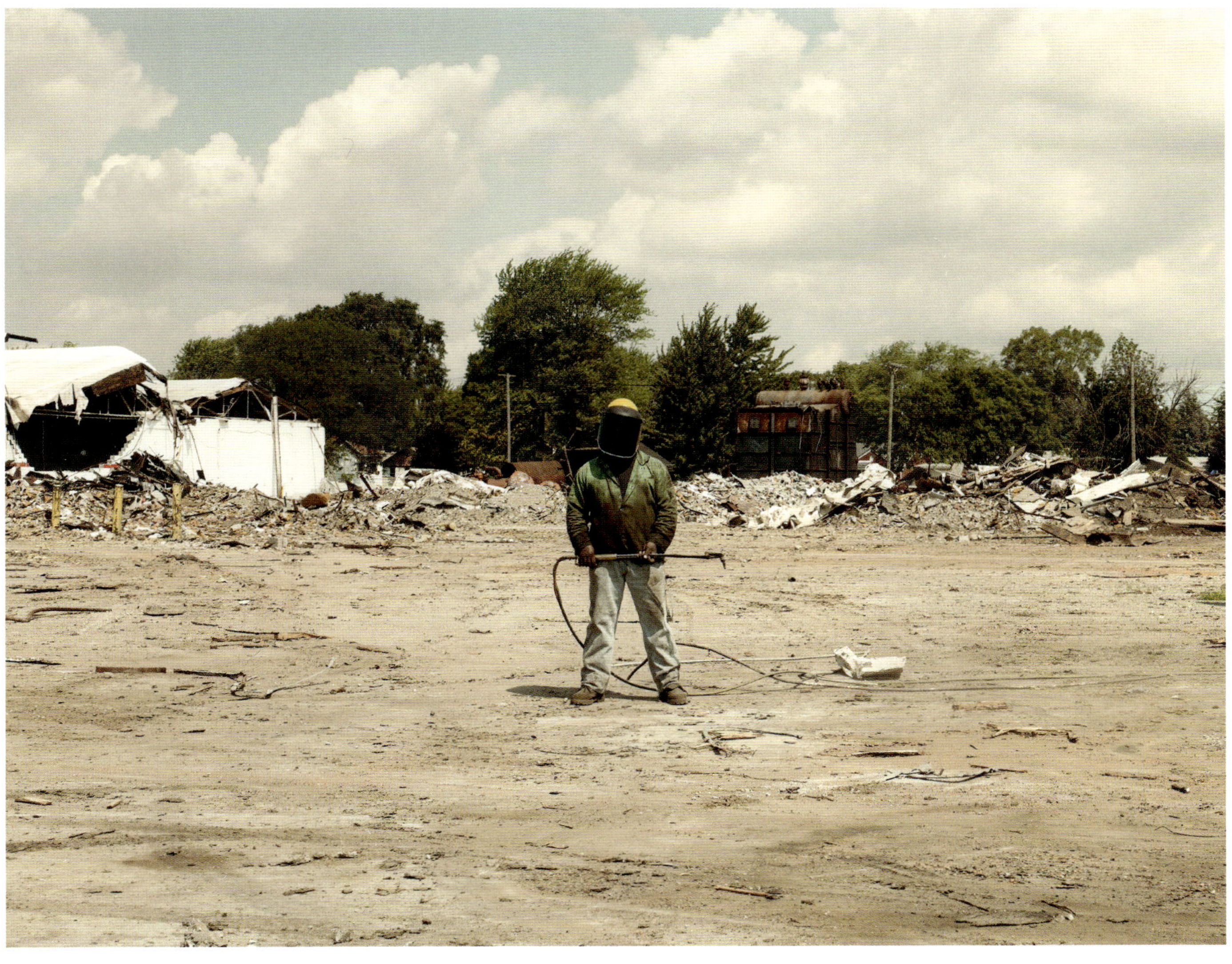

San Diego Bay Coastal Wetland Restoration
San Diego, California

Under this component, 230 acres of existing salt ponds, located on the west side of the Otay River channel, would be restored to shallow subtidal and intertidal habitat.

Amount funded by Recovery Act: $2,900,000.00

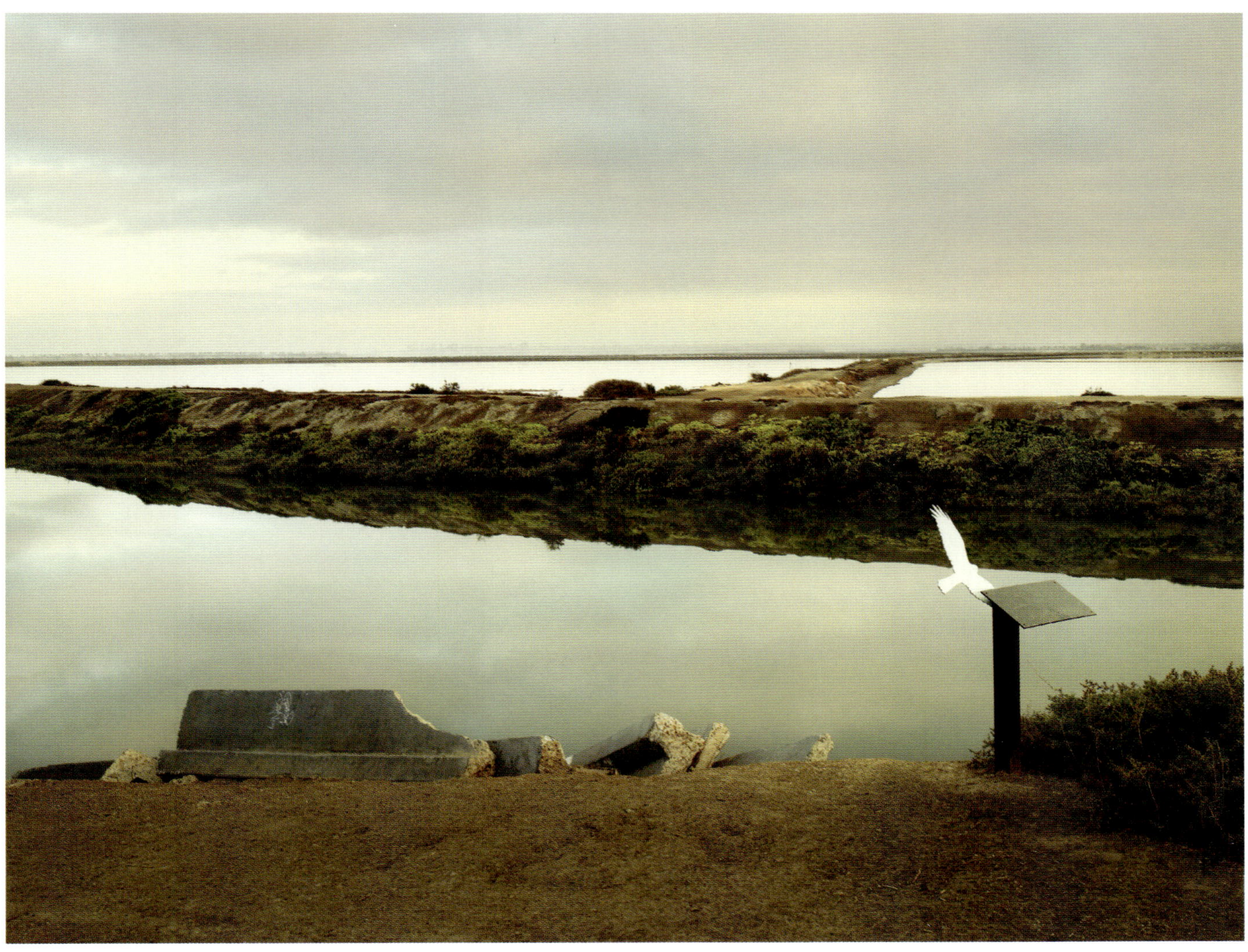

Cochiti Lake
Albuquerque, New Mexico

Campground Construction Phase III. Backlog Infrastructure
Maintenance Issue—the aging and obsolete existing campground
no longer supports current recreational interests and needs and
therefore must be modernized. Completion of campground is
essential to public welfare.

Amount funded by Recovery Act: $2,380,000.00

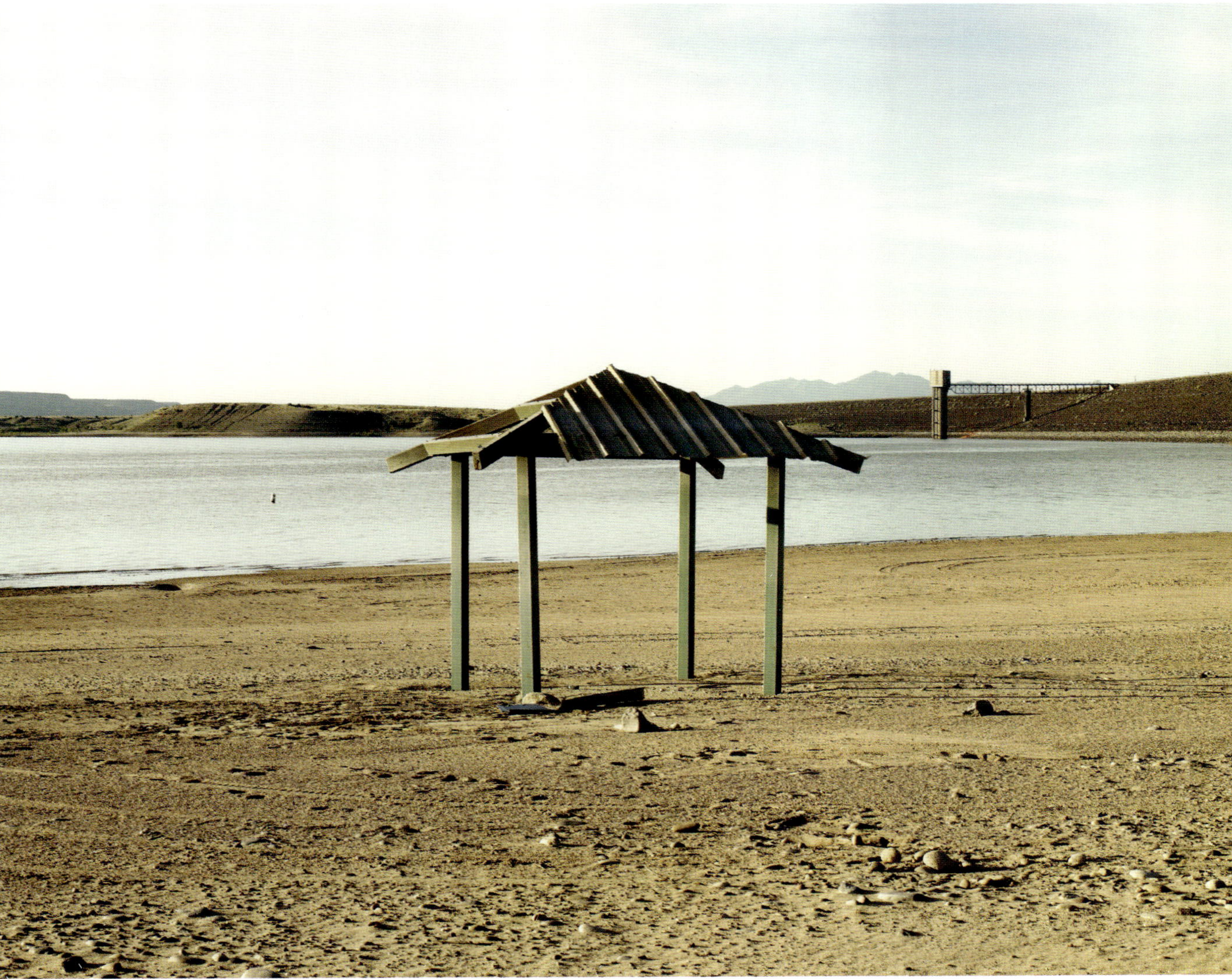

Lower Mission Creek Investigation
Santa Barbara, California

Fully fund architect/engineer contract to prepare plans
and specifications for the construction on the lower half of
Mission Creek.

Amount funded by Recovery Act: $600,000.00

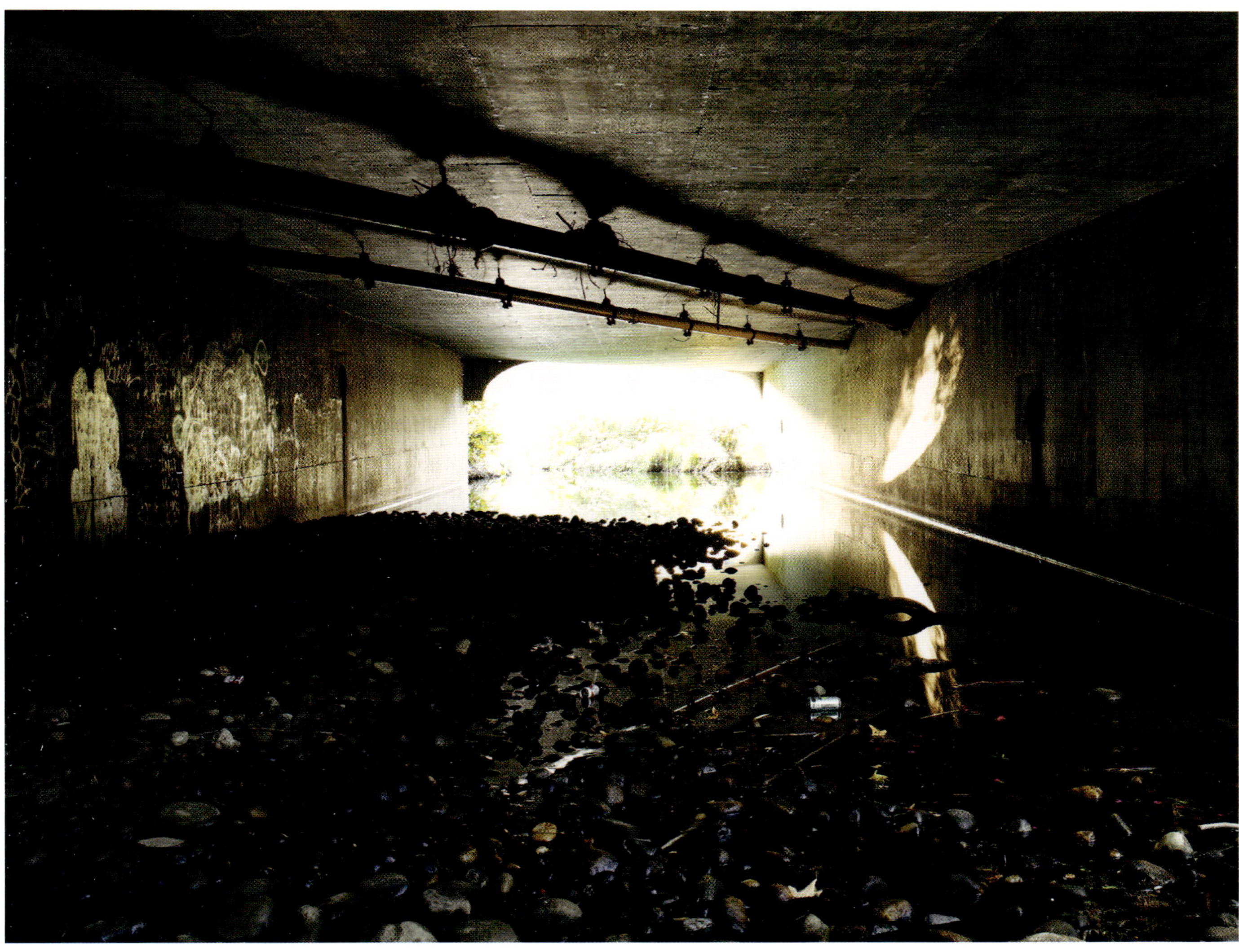

Joint Force Headquarters
Raleigh, North Carolina

Construction of Joint Force Headquarters. Electrical duct
bank, concrete footings, sitework (erosion control, grading,
clearing and grading, stormwater drainage).

Amount funded by Recovery Act: $24,382,110.00

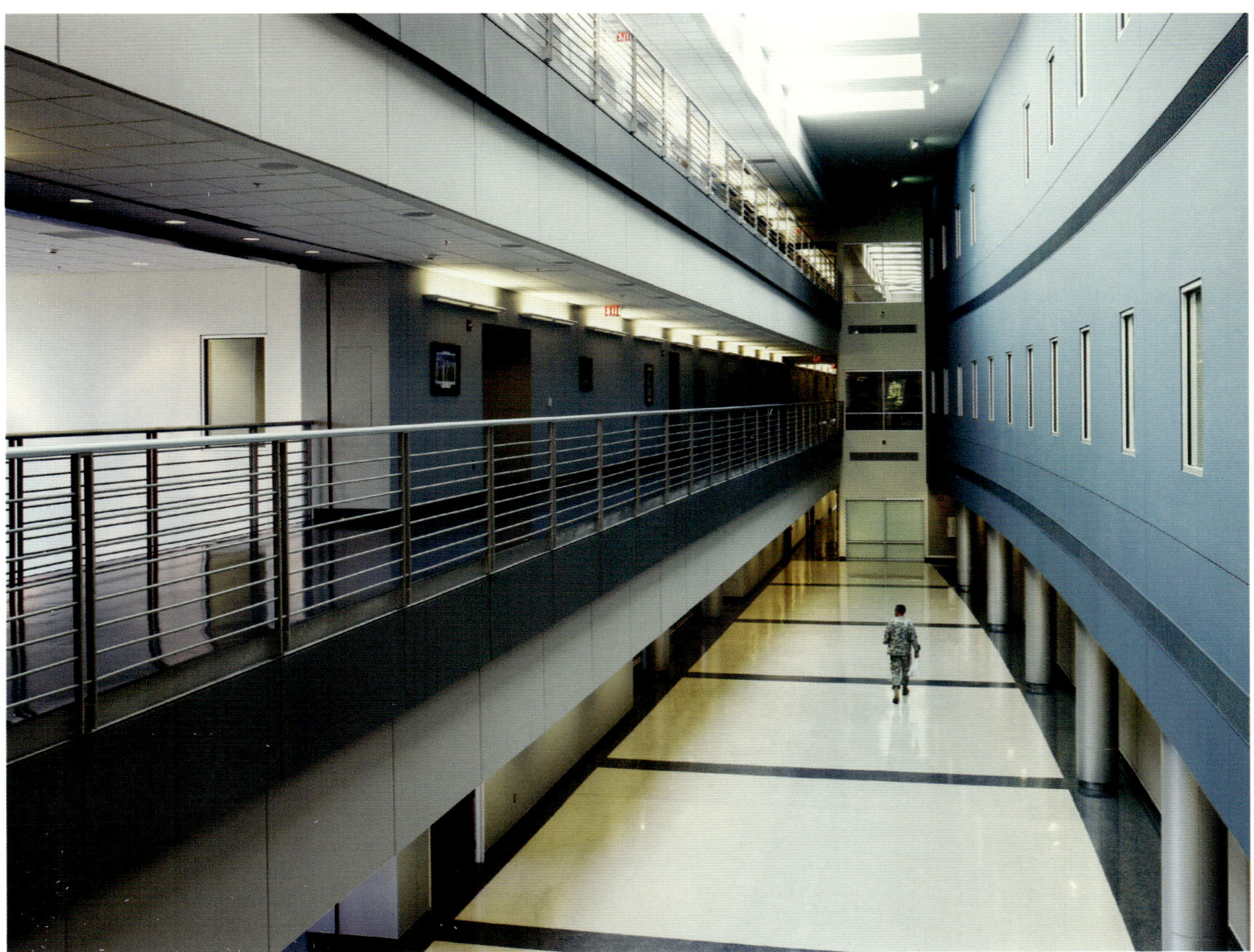

Fullerton Dam
Fullerton, California

Construct log boom at Fullerton Dam to keep debris from
reaching the intake tower, improve drainage in the dam
reservoir and prevent large debris from entering the trash racks
and/or flood control gates at the intake tower and causing a
possible stoppage.

Amount funded by Recovery Act: $815,000.00

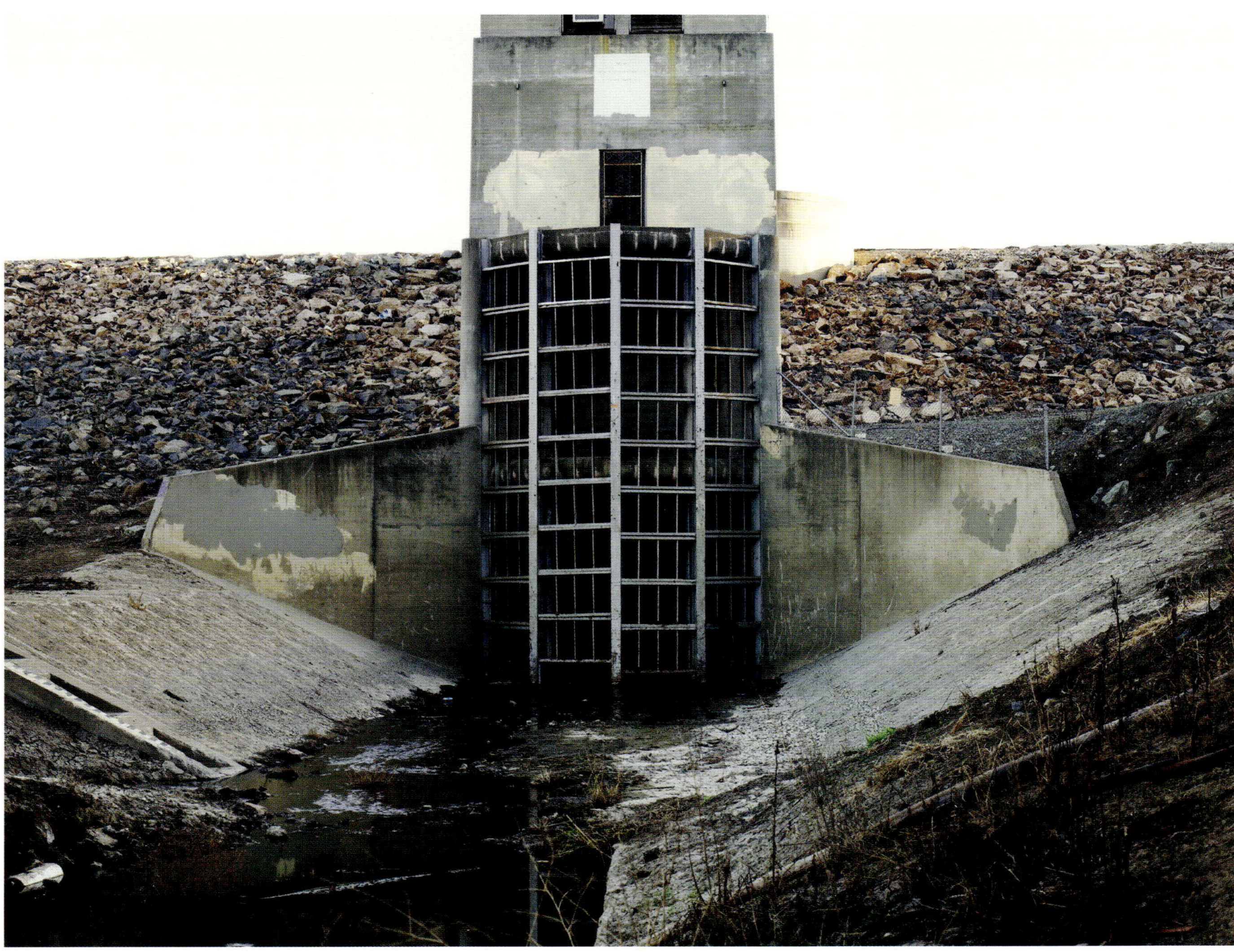

New Hogan Lake
Valley Springs, California

Install shade shelters in Oak Knoll Campground. Shade tress
are lacking due to water fluctuations. Renovate picnic tables.
Project will reduce future maintenance and enhance visitor
satisfaction.

Amount funded by Recovery Act: $275,000.00

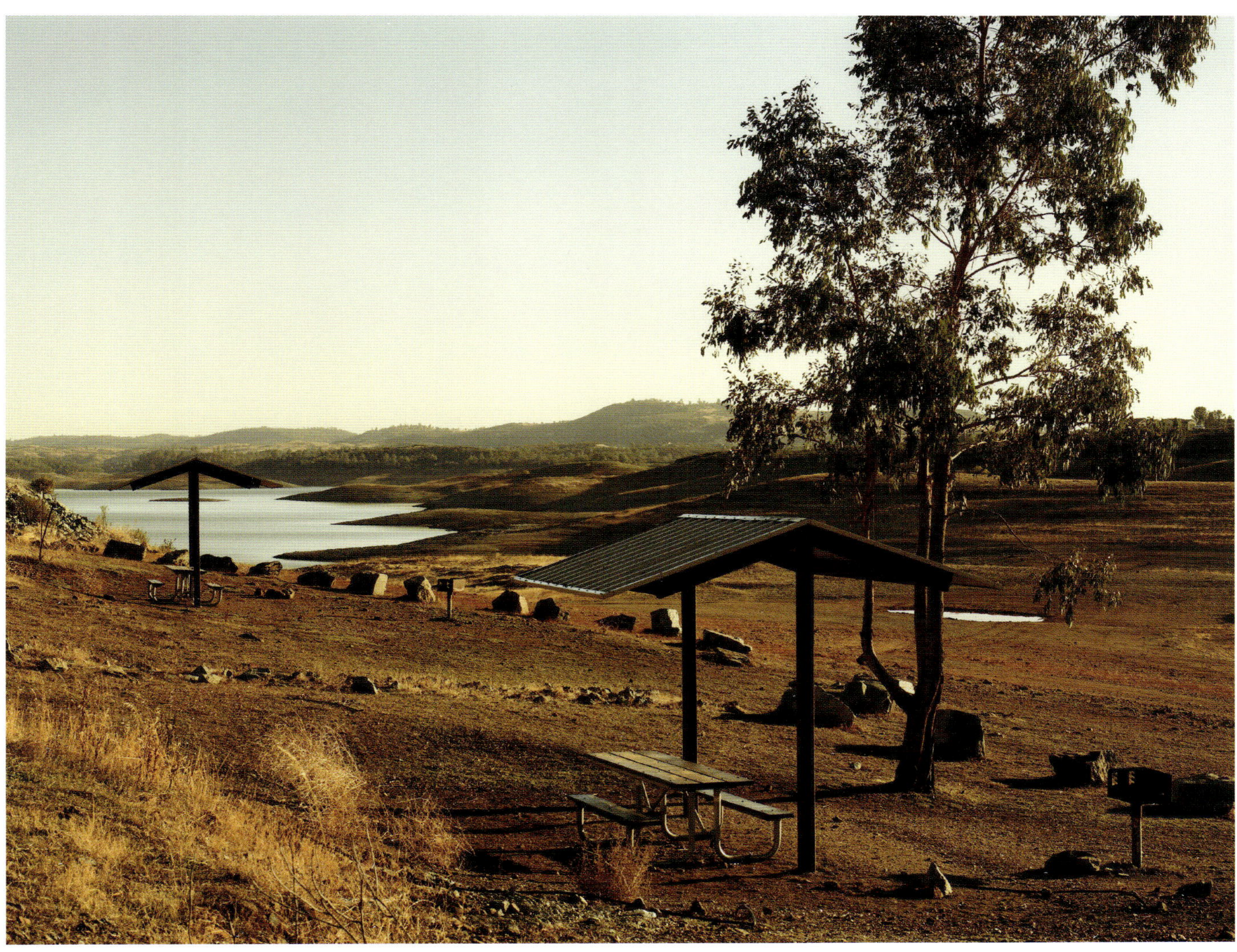

Los Angeles County Drainage Area
Los Angeles, California

Removal of graffiti. Grafitti abatement on the channel walls of the Santa Ana River Basin is an exponentially growing manpower and resource requirement which cannot be met with current resources and directly affects the communities along the flood drainage area.

Amount funded by Recovery Act: $900,000.00

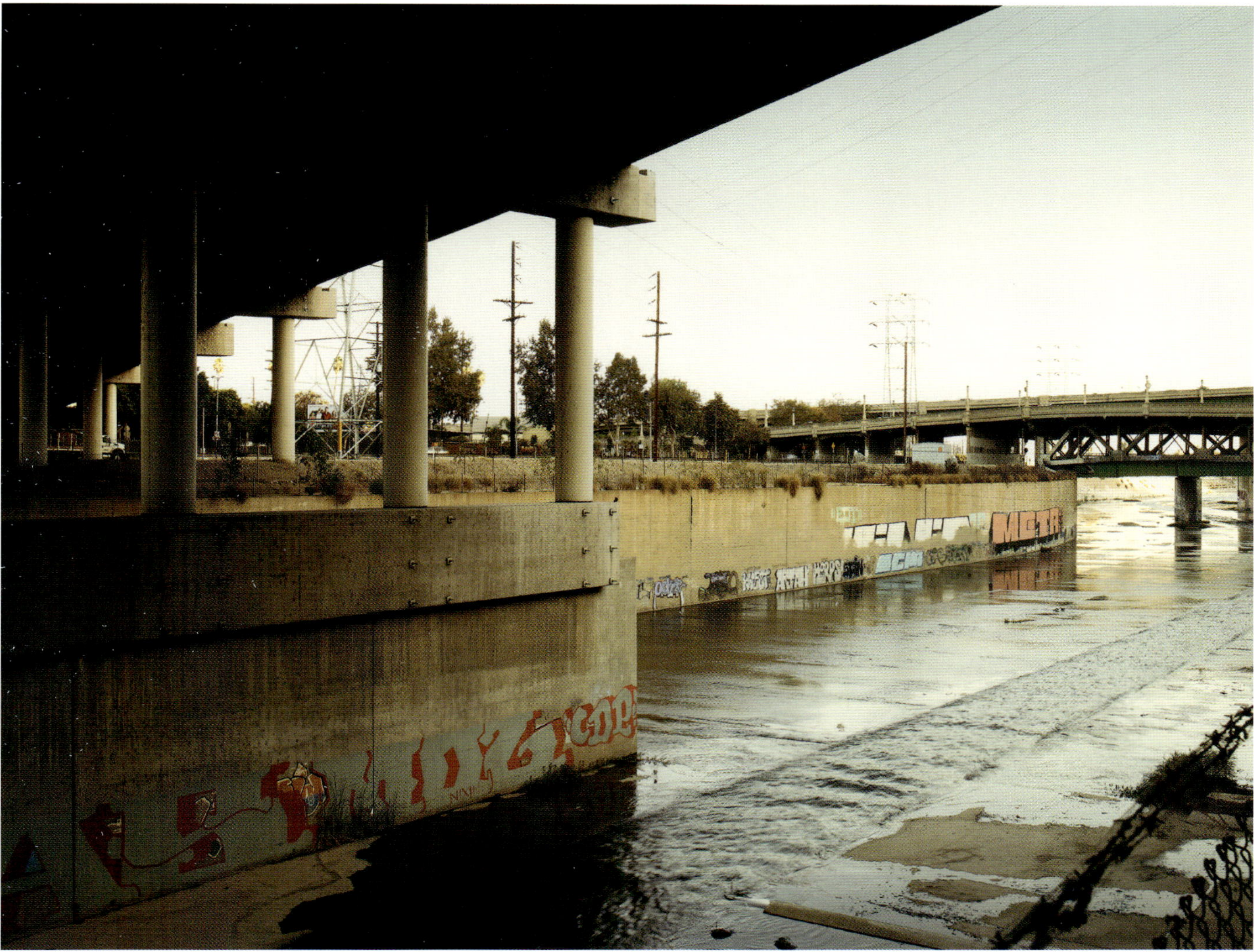

Cachuma Lake County Park
Santa Barbara, California

This project is for the upgrade of the Mohawk Area Restrooms
to bring the facility into compliance with the American
Disabilities Act.

Amount funded by Recovery Act: $487,000.00

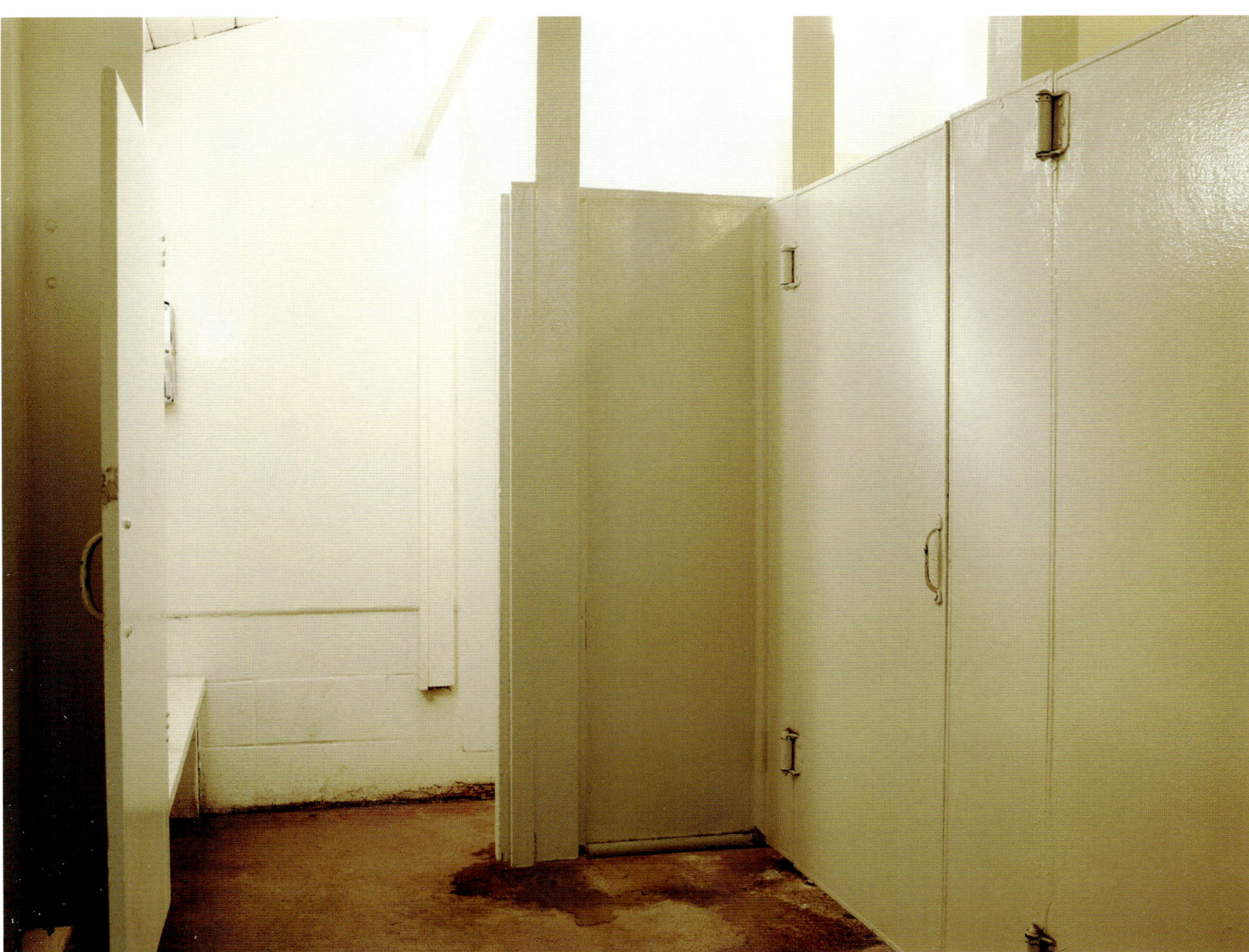

Gold Coast Transit
Ventura County, California

Funds granted for purchases of buses and equipment.

Amount funded by Recovery Act: $4,393,000.00

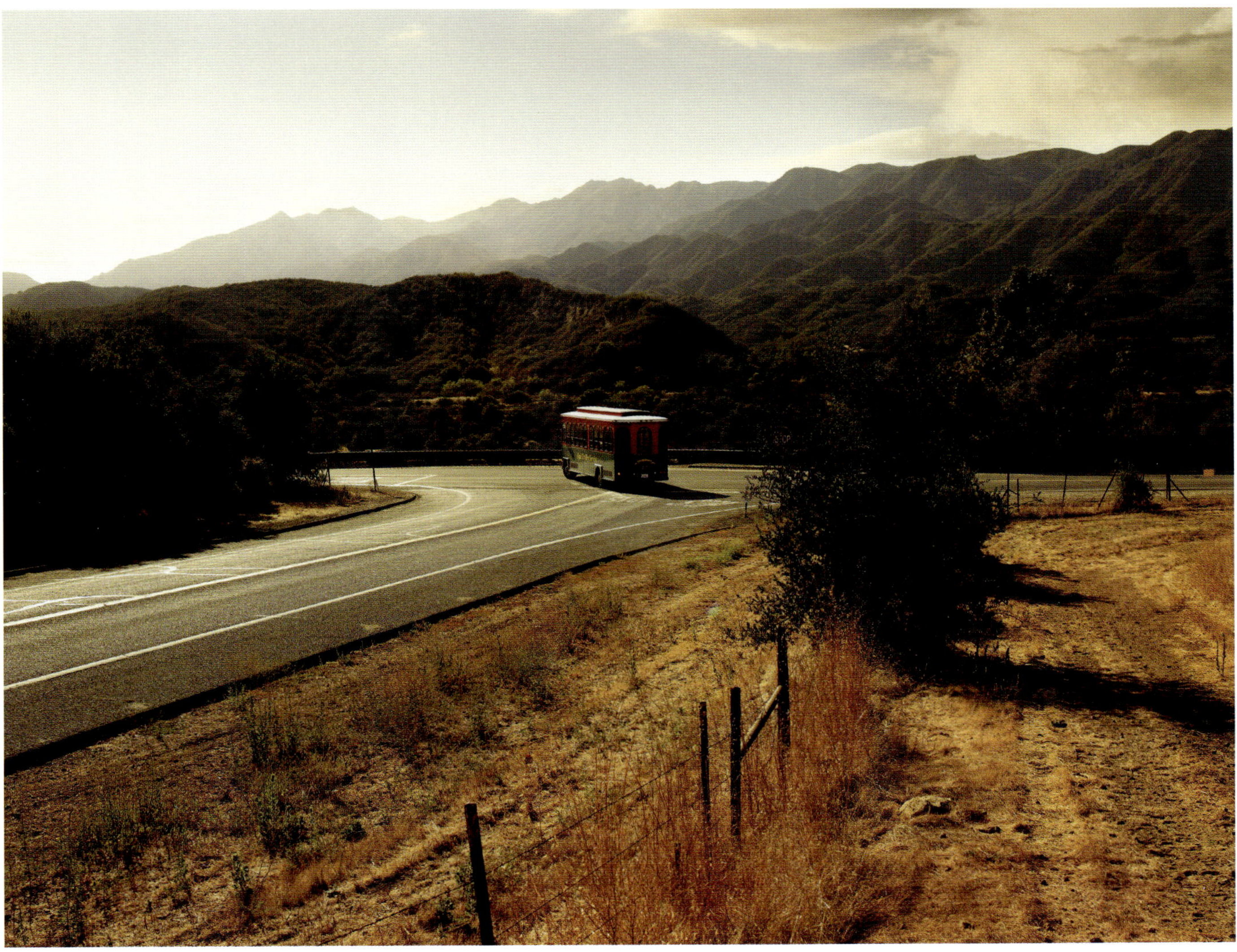

City of Simi Valley
Simi Valley, California

Funds granted for purchases of shelters and buses, and ADA operations.

Amount funded by Recovery Act: $2,015,700.00

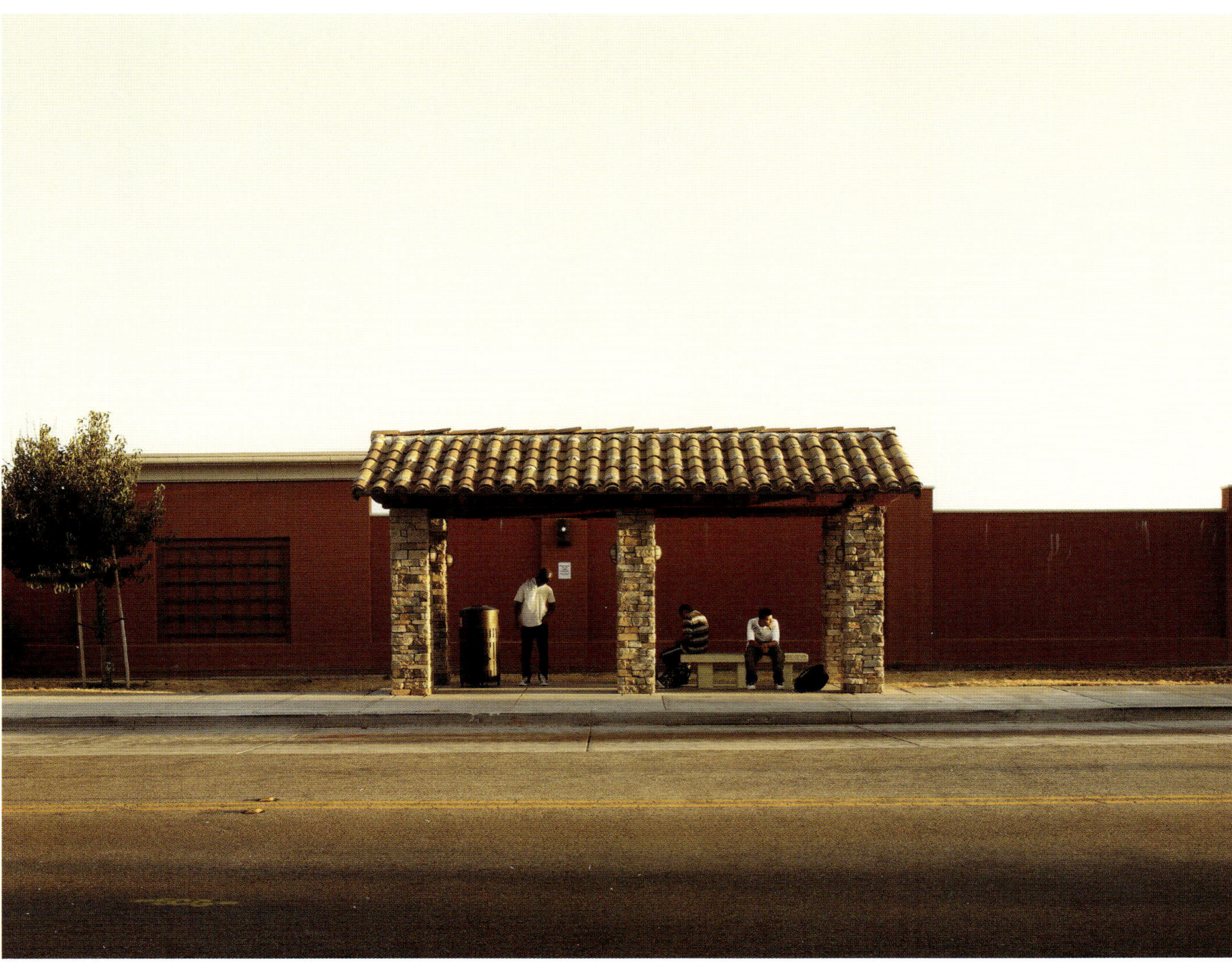

Boysville of Michigan
Detroit, Michigan

Title I—Part D Delinquent Institutions.

Amount funded by Recovery Act: $131,435.00

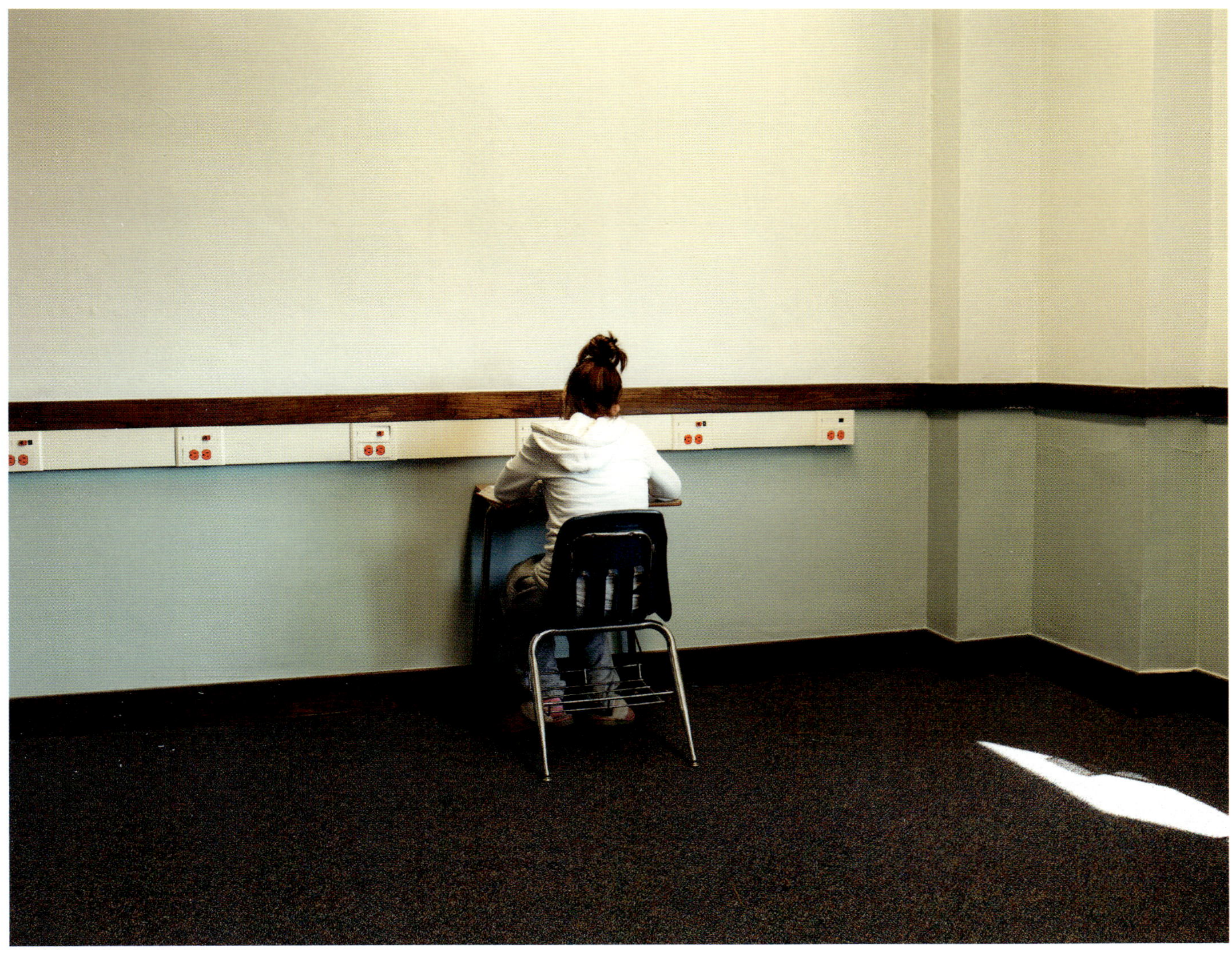

Rose Creek Bike/Pedestrian Bridge
San Diego, California

Funds allocated for construction of a bike/pedestrian bridge to connect with the existing bike path and provide access across Rose Creek.

Amount funded by Recovery Act: $5,000,000.00

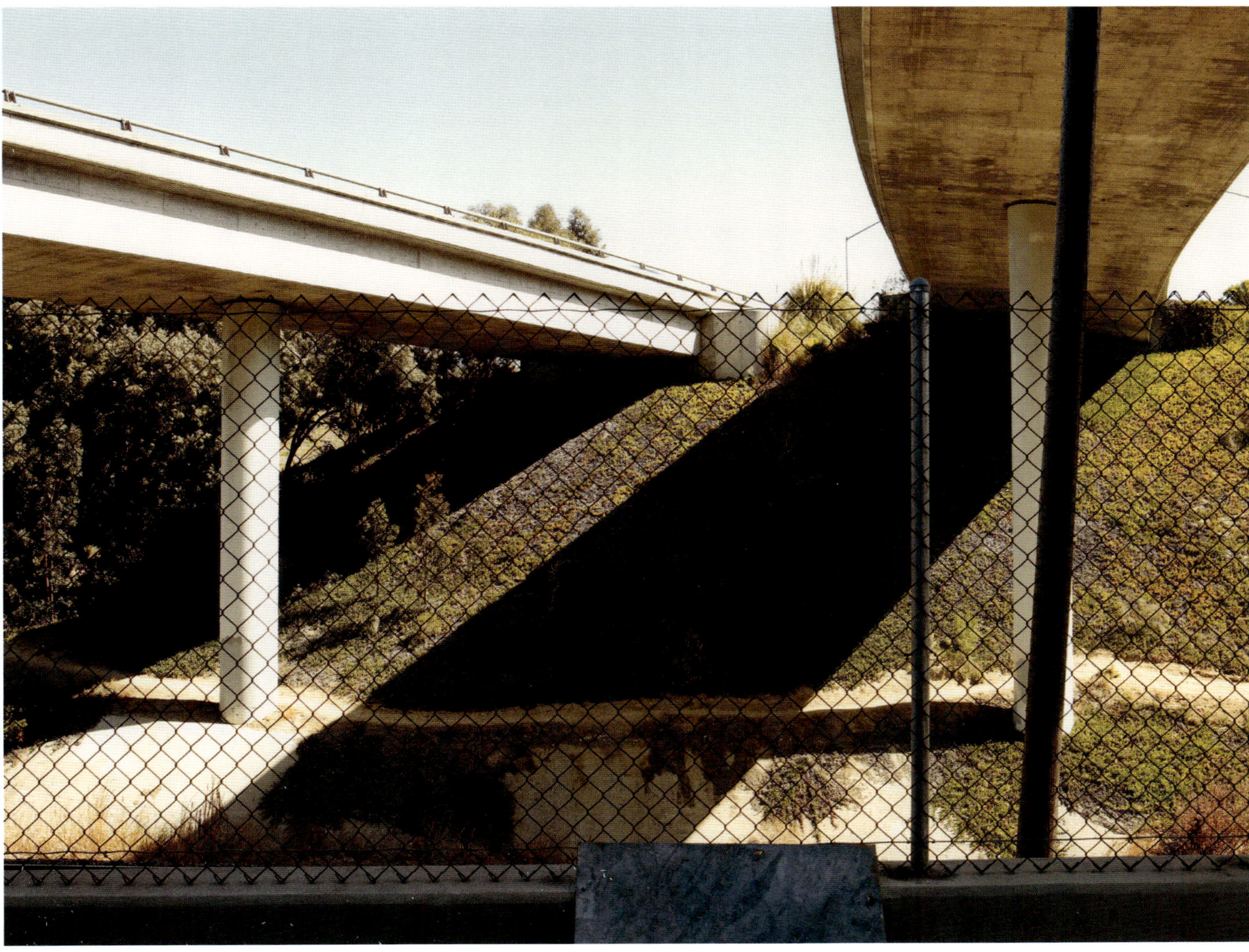

Housing Authority of The City of San Buena Ventura
San Buena Ventura, California

Santa Clara Apartments Green Retrofit. Conduct energy efficient upgrades to existing public housing community. This funding can be expected to result in providing employment to architects and engineers, construction workers, and product manufacturers.

Amount funded by Recovery Act: $331,967.00

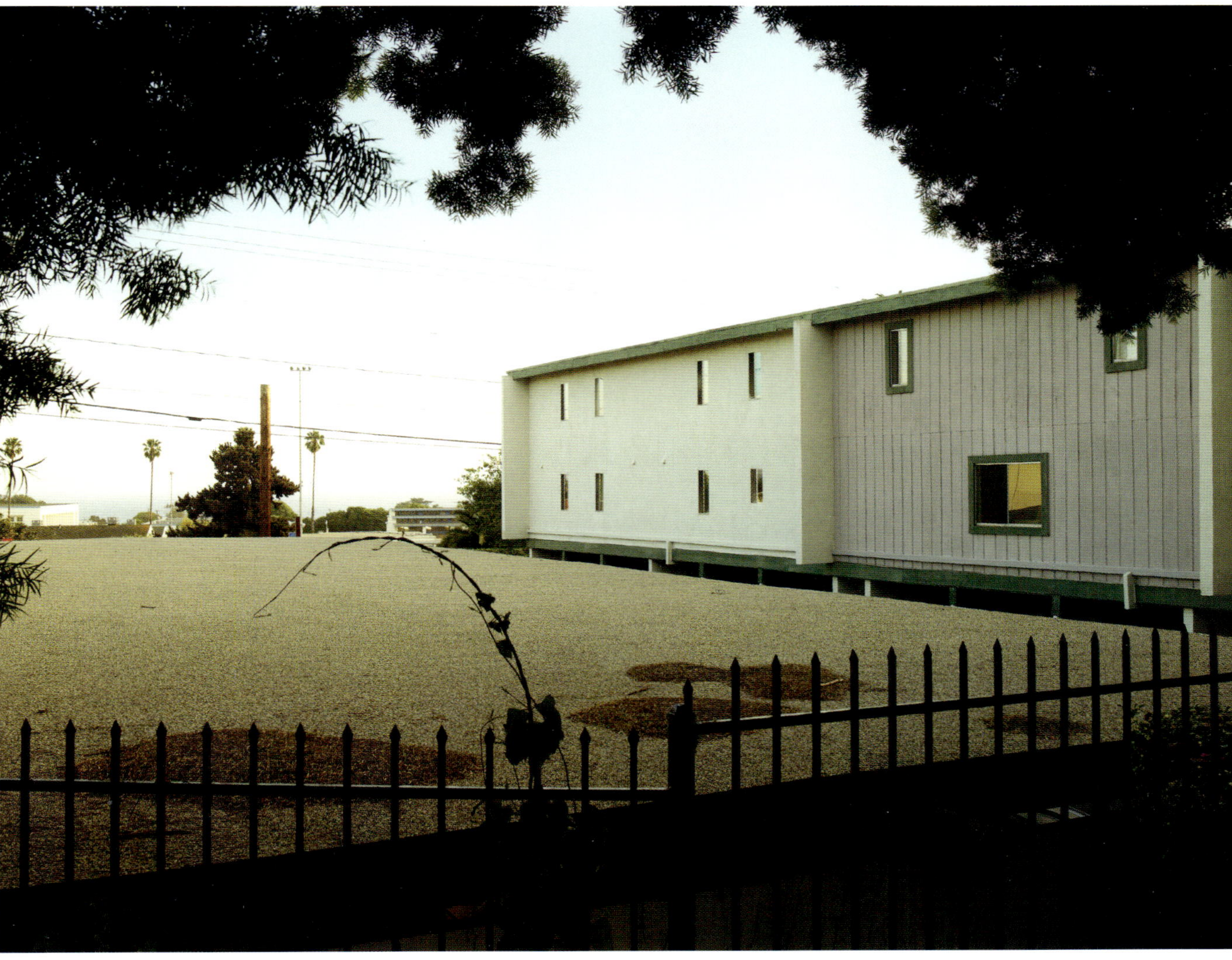

Santa Ana River Mainstem
Chino, California

Complete contract for channel improvements to Reach 9 Phase 2B of the lower Santa Ana River.

Amount funded by Recovery Act: $26,000,000.00

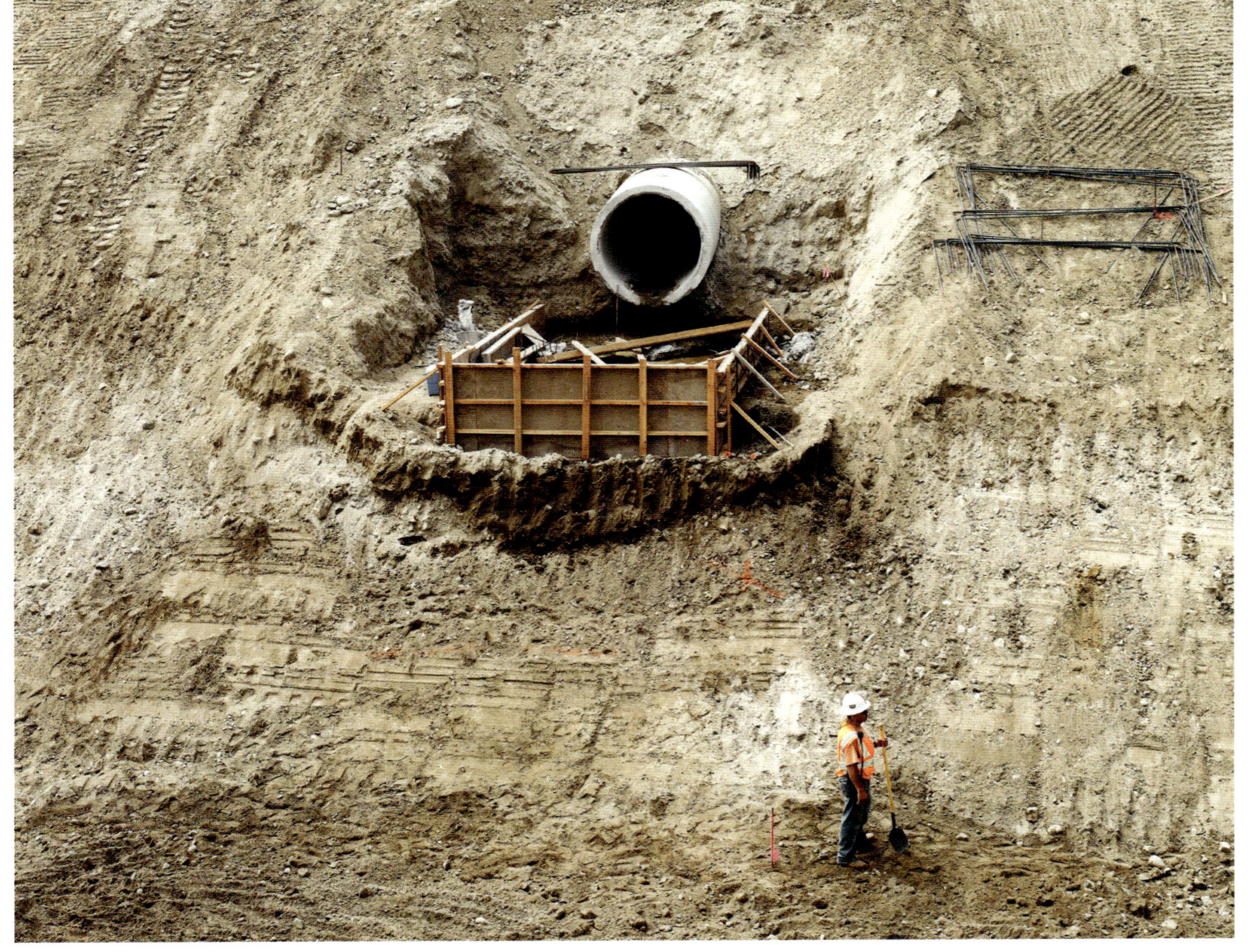

Santa Maria River Levee Reinforcement
Santa Maria, California

Project consists of reinforcement of 7 miles of levee with soil treatment and sheetpile. The U.S. Army Corps of Engineers will be the responsible agency for this project. Santa Barbara County will assist the Corps with land rights and utilities.

Amount funded by Recovery Act: $40,230,000.00

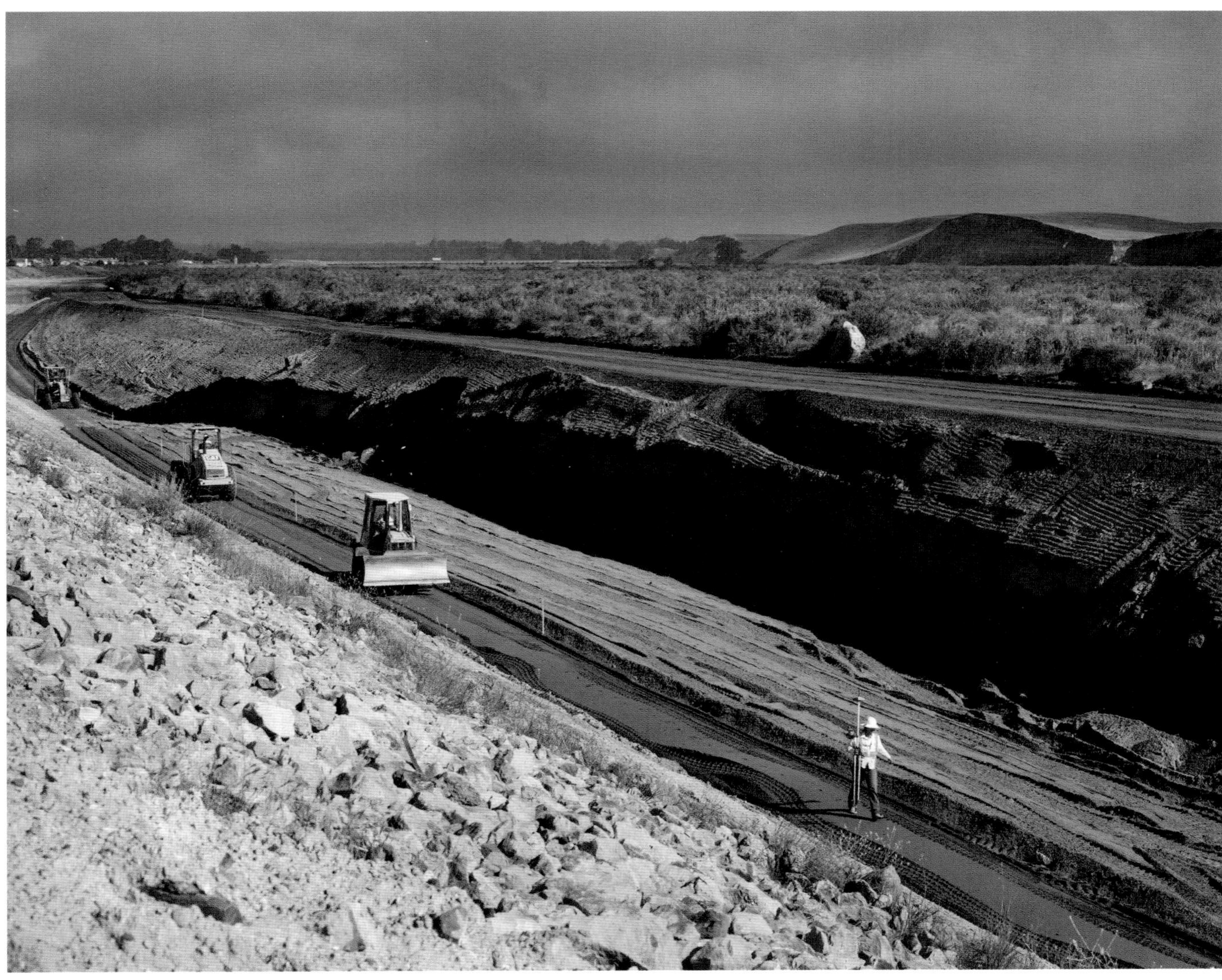

Neighborhood Stabilization Program
Detroit, Michigan
(TWO IMAGES)

Within the 140 mile area of the City of Detroit, officials
estimate that there are approximately 33,000 vacant homes
and 90,000 empty lots. In 2009, the City of Detroit demolished
860 vacant homes and aims to demolish thousands more
during 2010 and over the next several years.

Amount funded by Recovery Act: $45,332,612.00

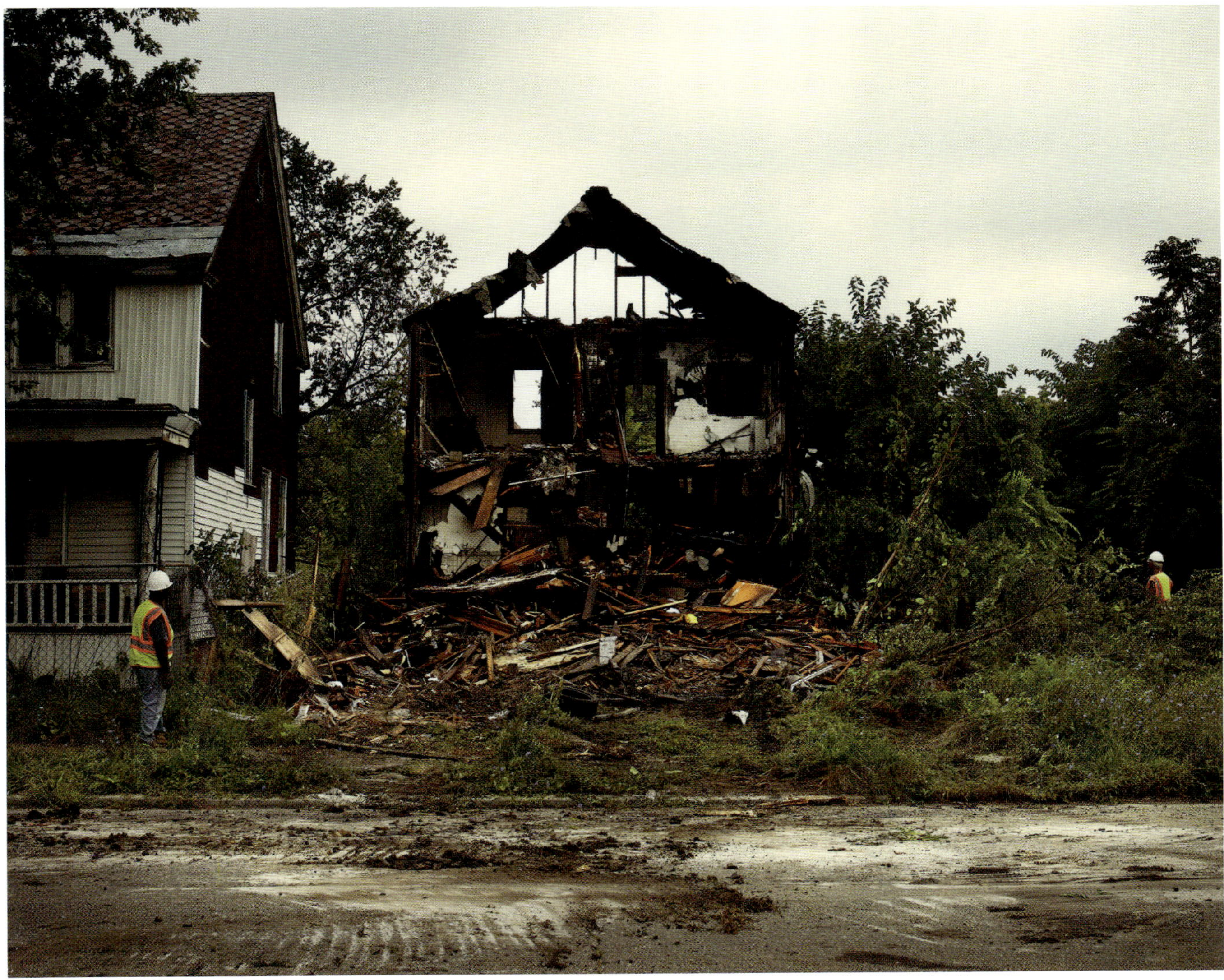

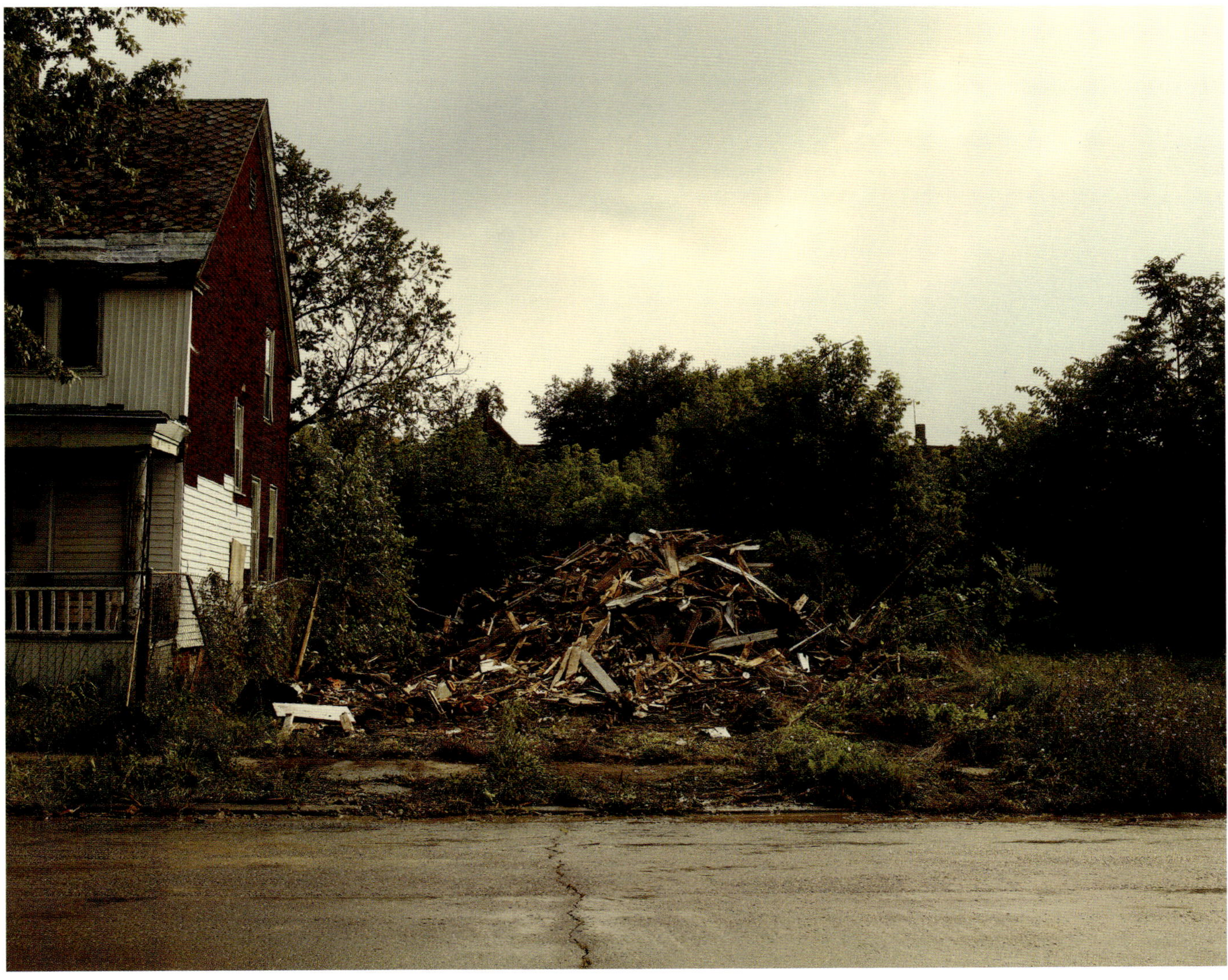

Cedar Gateway Apartments
San Diego, California

The U.S. Department of Housing & Urban Development
(HUD) provided grant funding to the California Tax Credit
Allocation Committee for capital investment in qualified Low
Income Housing Tax Credit (LIHTC) projects.

Amount funded by Recovery Act: $14,024,415.00

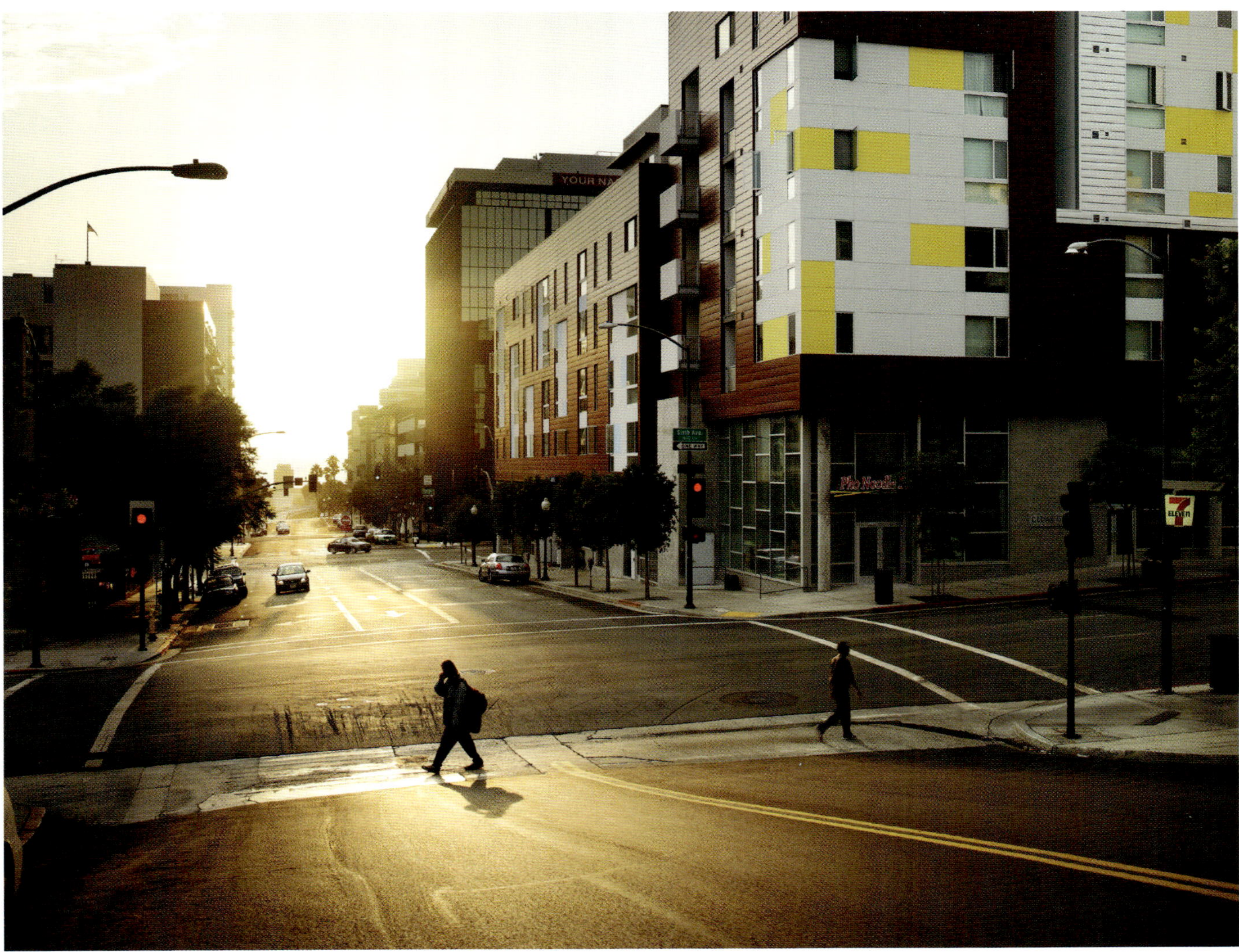

Brownfields Redevelopment Program
Jackson, Michigan

157,000 square feet with 14 acres heavy industrial former plastigage facility located in Blackman Charter Township at 2917 Wildwood Avenue. Most buildings will be demolished and will be ready for redevelopment.

Amount funded by Recovery Act: $1,000,000.00

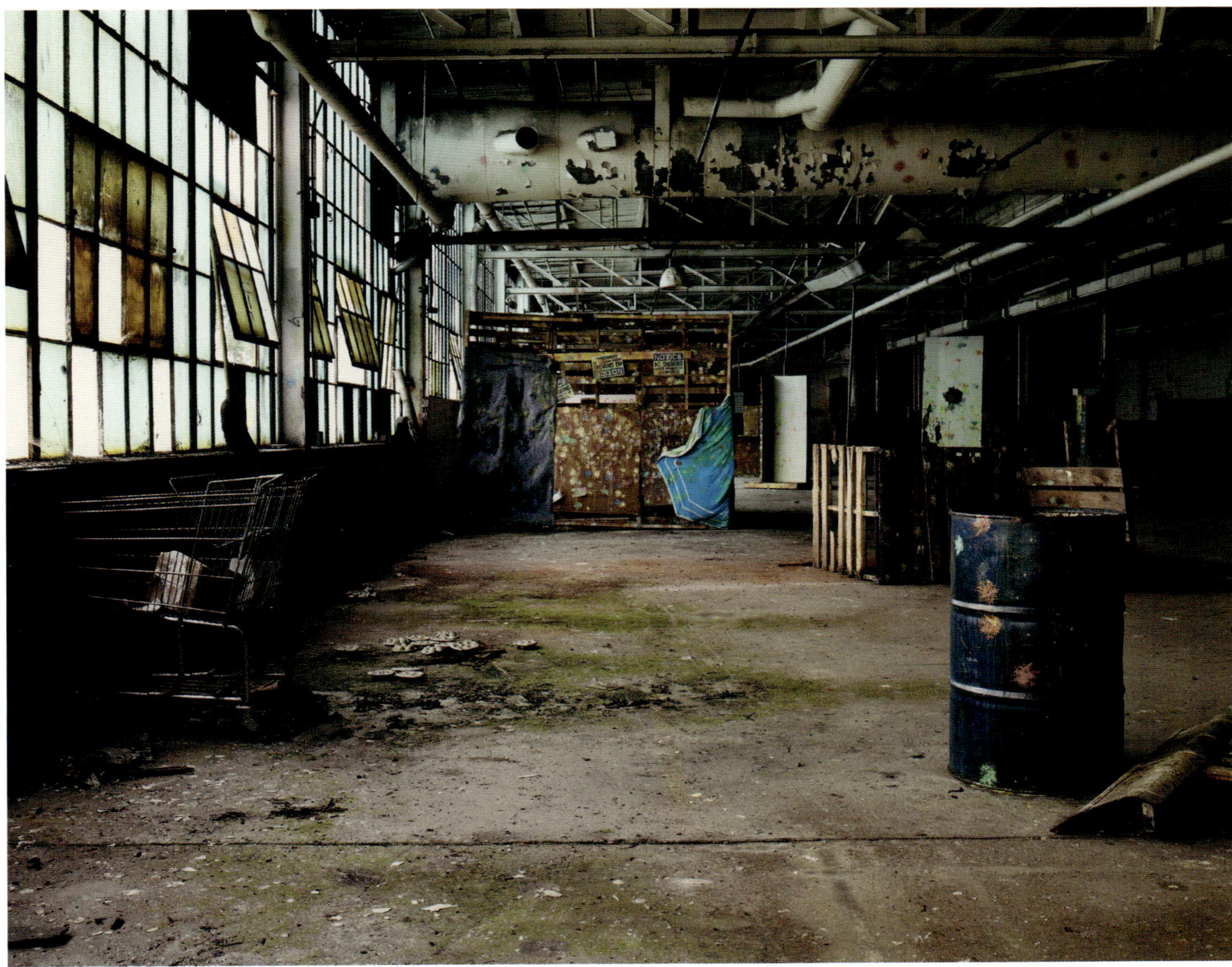

Brownfields
Lincoln Park, Michigan

The City plans to use the grant to develop an inventory of
Brownfields within the Community, and then perform
environmental assessments on priority sites to identify issues of
concern and help prepare them for sale and/or redevelopment.

Amout funded by Recovery Act: $200,000.00

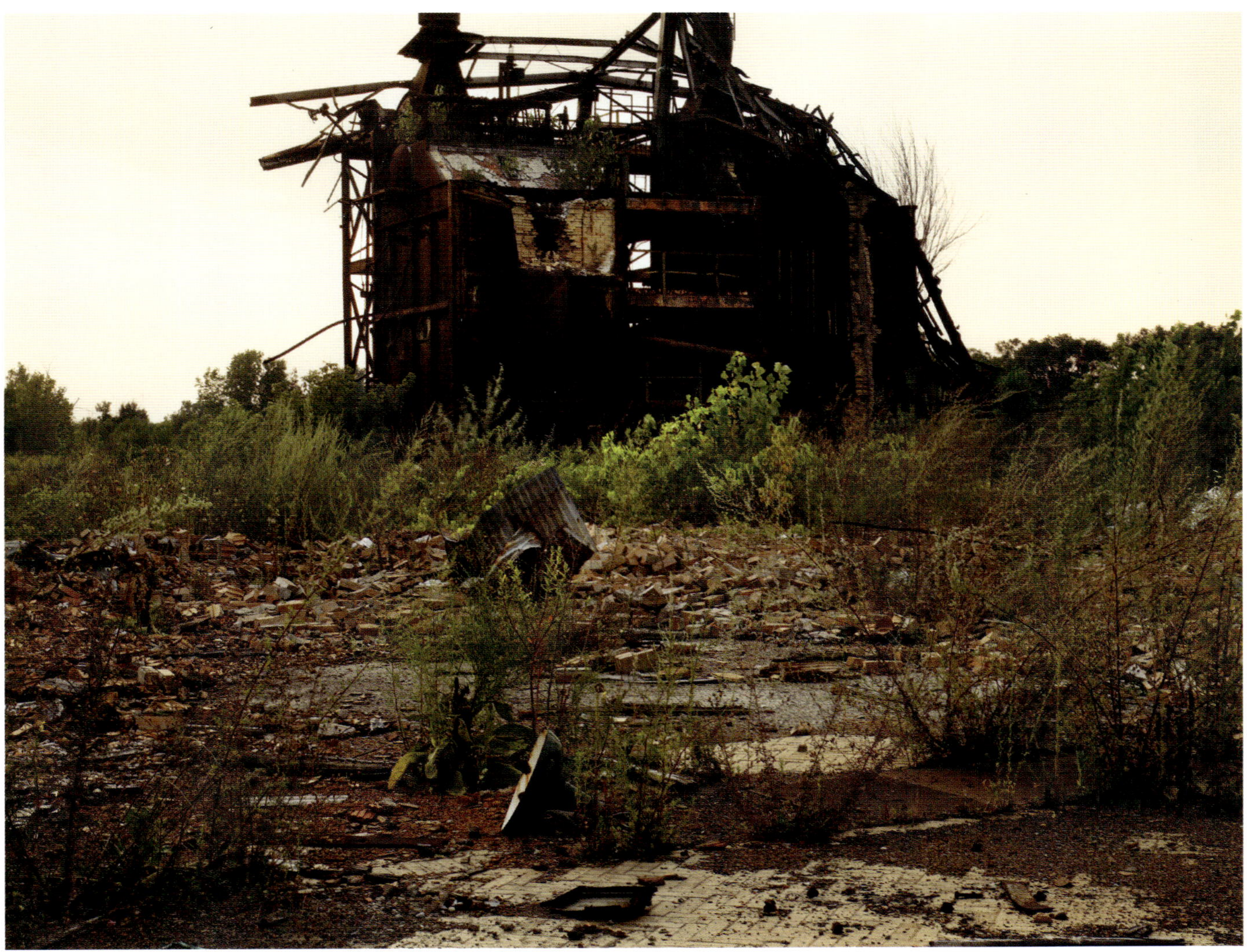

Sheet Metal Workers Local 80
Warren, Michigan

International Training Institute for Sheet Metal and Air Conditioning Industry: funds used for training workers in both Washentenaw and Macomb counties.

Amount funded by Recovery Act: $1,000,000.00

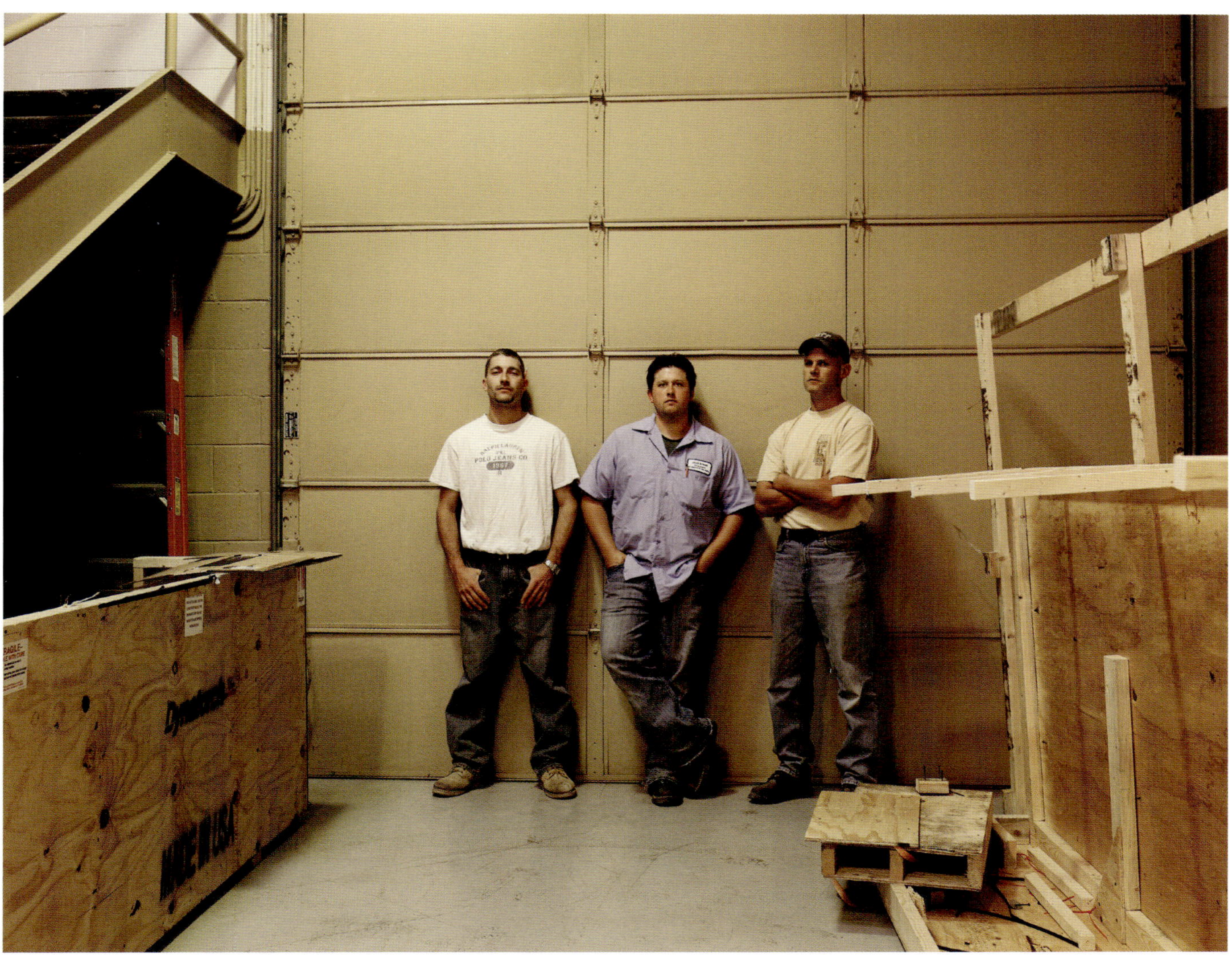

Universtiy of Michigan
Ann Arbor, Michigan
(TWO IMAGES)

The primary goal of this proposal is to computerize taxonomic, geographic, and stratigraphic information for catalogued invertebrate fossils at the University of Michigan Museum of Paleontology (UMMP-IC). The online database will be available to the general public.

Amount funded by Recovery Act: $304,867.00

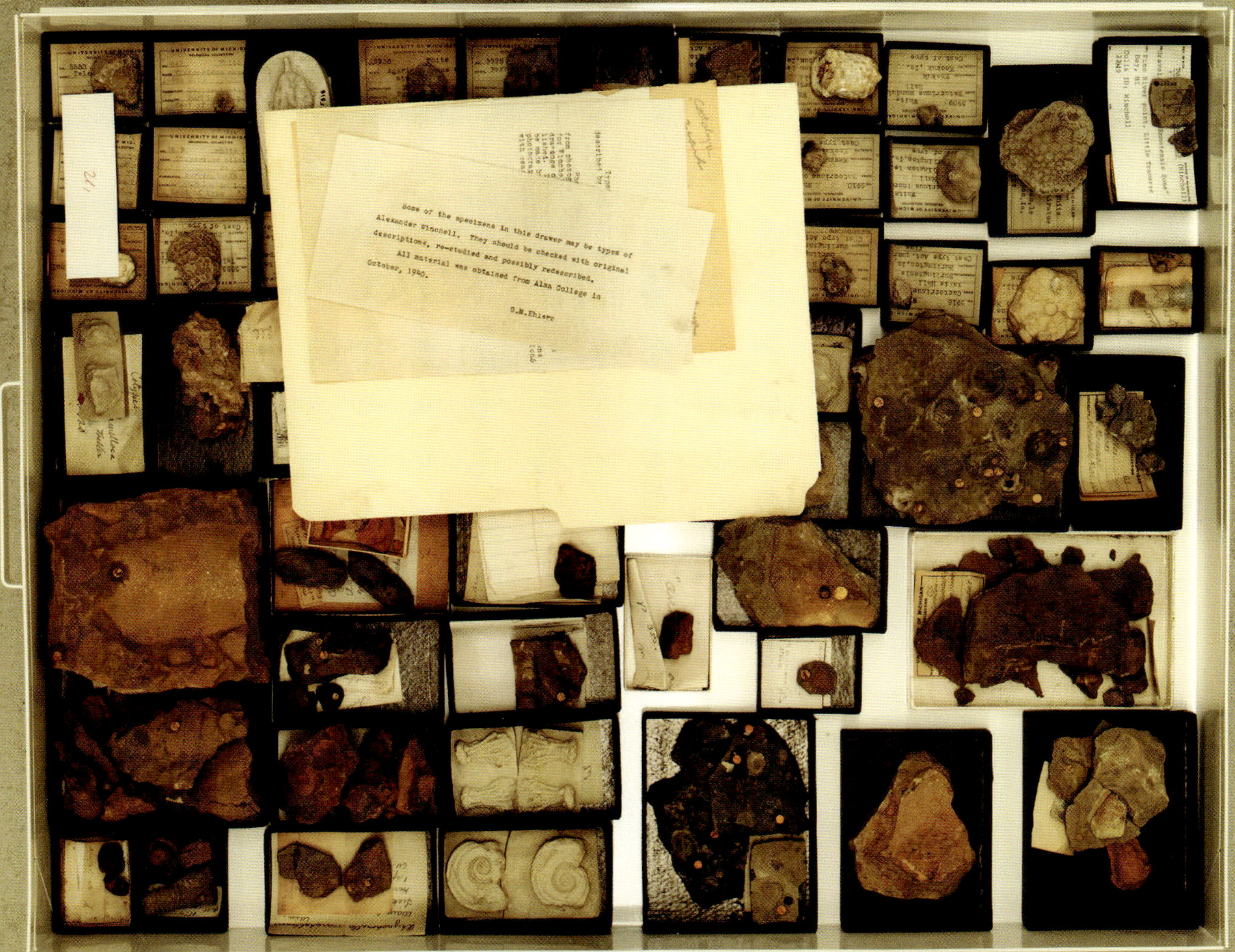
Some of the specimens in this drawer may be types of
Alexander Winchell. They should be checked with original
descriptions, re-studied and possibly redescribed.
All material was obtained from Alma College in
October, 1940.
G.M.Ehlers

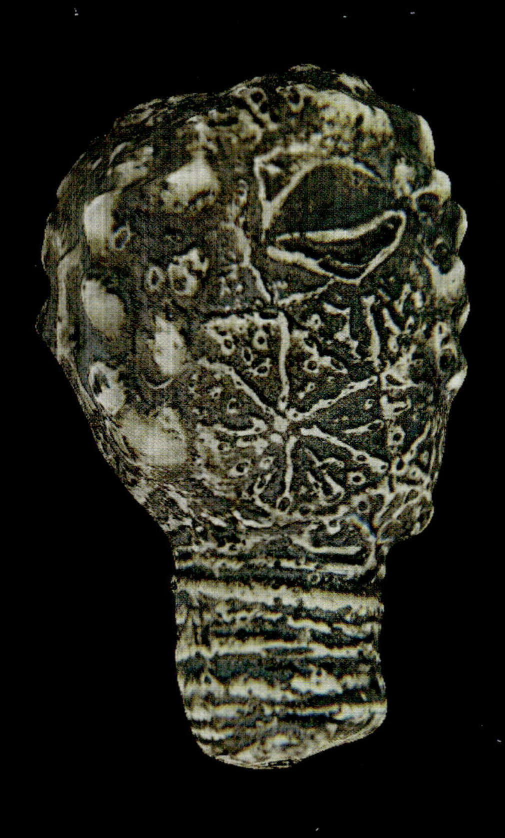

City Of Kentwood
Grand Rapids, Michigan

Award Grant to the City of Kentwood Michigan for lighting upgrades to Kentwood's campus parking lot and customer-owned street to LED lighting.

Amount funded by Recovery Act: $217,900.00

Santa Ana River Mainstem
Chino, California

Complete contract for channel improvements to Reach 9
Phase 2B of the lower Santa Ana River.

Amount funded by Recovery Act: $26,000,000.00

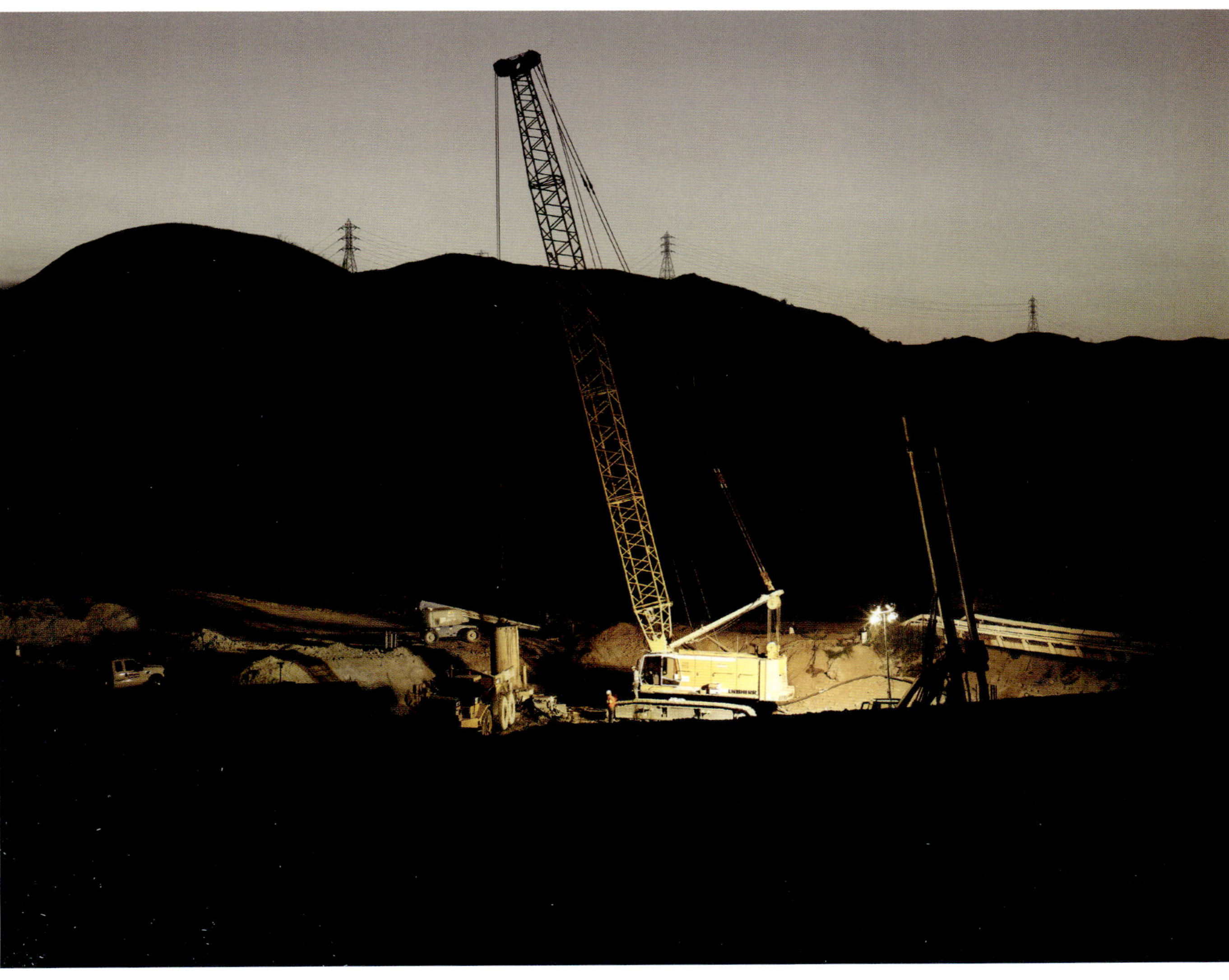

Santa Ynez Shoulder Widening
Santa Ynez, California

Widen Refugio Road and Roblar Avenue to provide shoulder enhancement to increase the safety for traveling public by increasing recovery zones for vehicles.

Amount funded by Recovery Act: $1,380,000.00

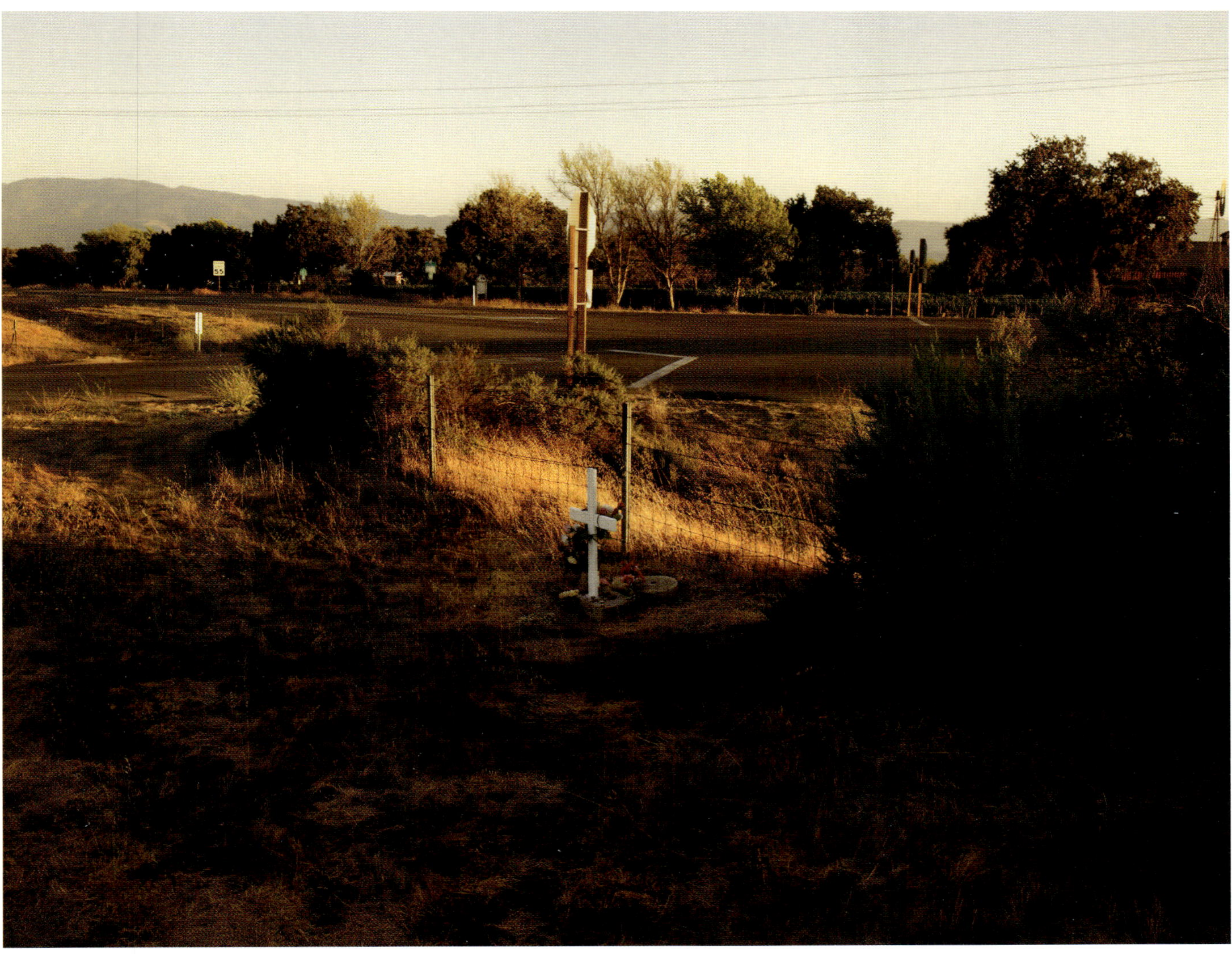

City of East Lansing
East Lansing, Michigan

The purpose of the project is to install infrastructure improvement, an alley, for a new housing project that includes both market rate and low moderate, income qualified households. The CDBG-R grant we received will be used entirely on the alley infrastructure improvements.

Amount funded by Recovery Act: $160,689.00

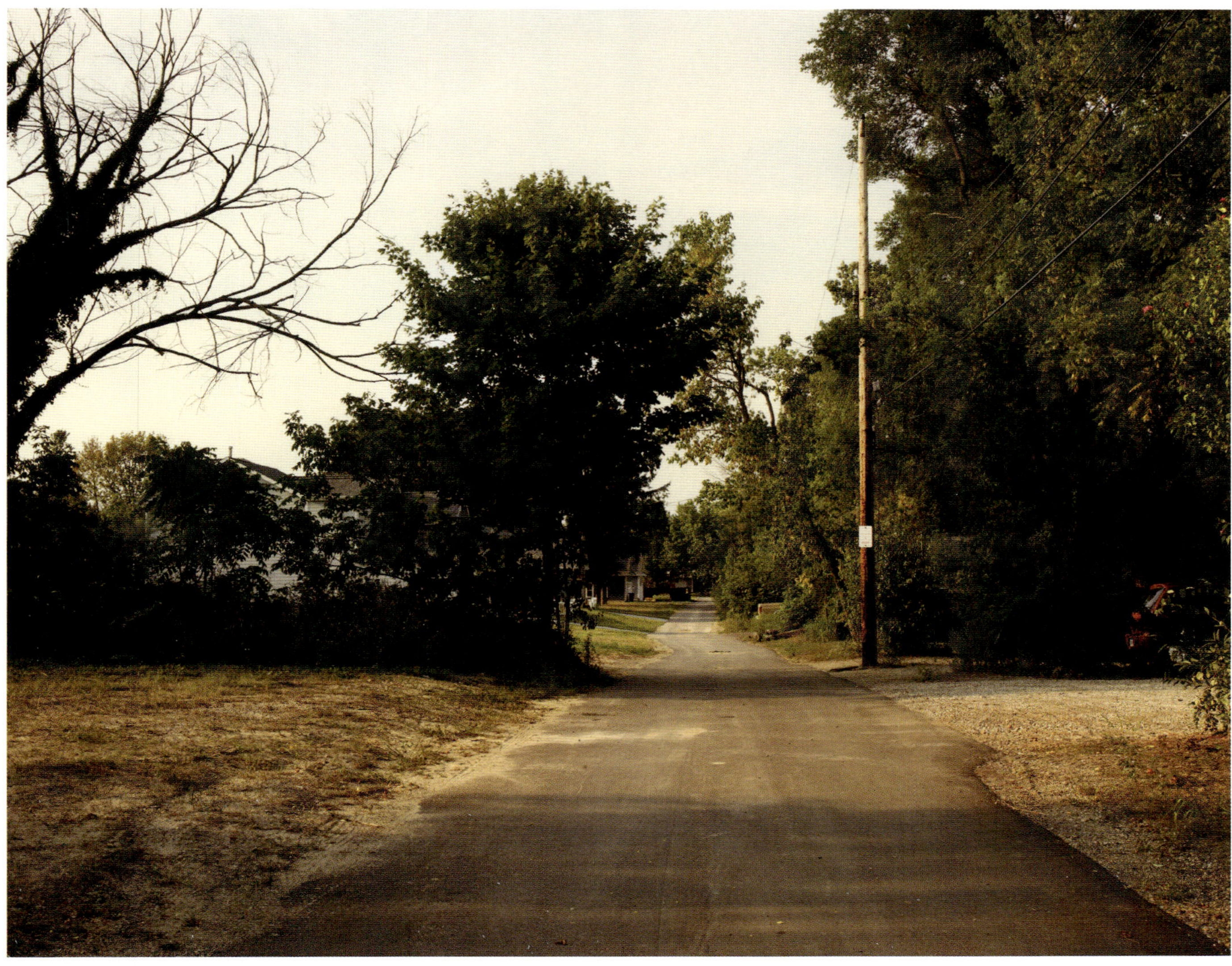

Santa Paula Creek
Santa Paula, California

Funds will be used to award 4 fully funded construction contracts to construct fish passage, complete required documentation, and complete project.

Amount funded by Recovery Act: $7,500,000.00

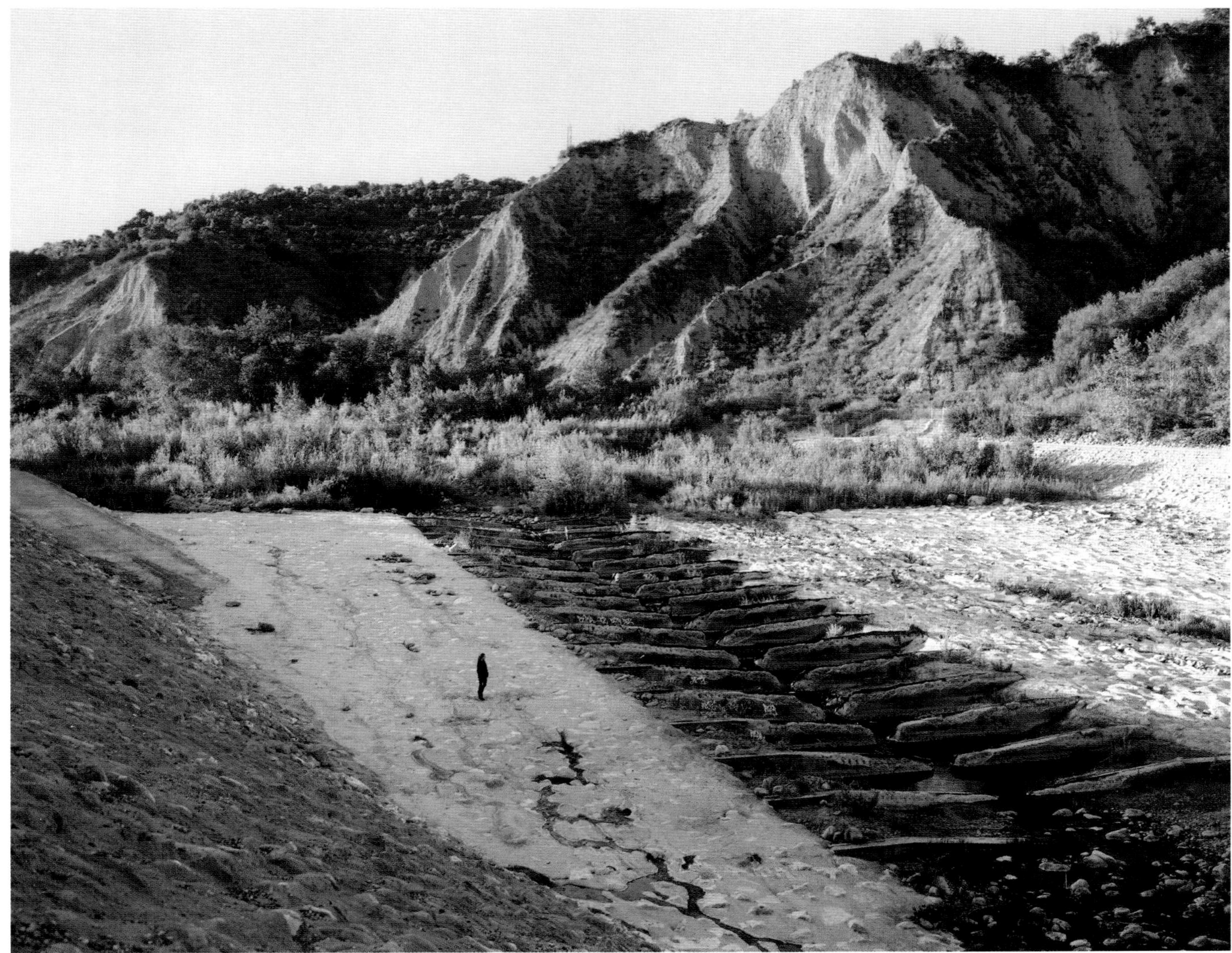

Muskegon Museum of Arts
Muskegon, Michigan

Funds used for temporary hiring of additional security guard.

Amount funded by Recovery Act: $14,900.00

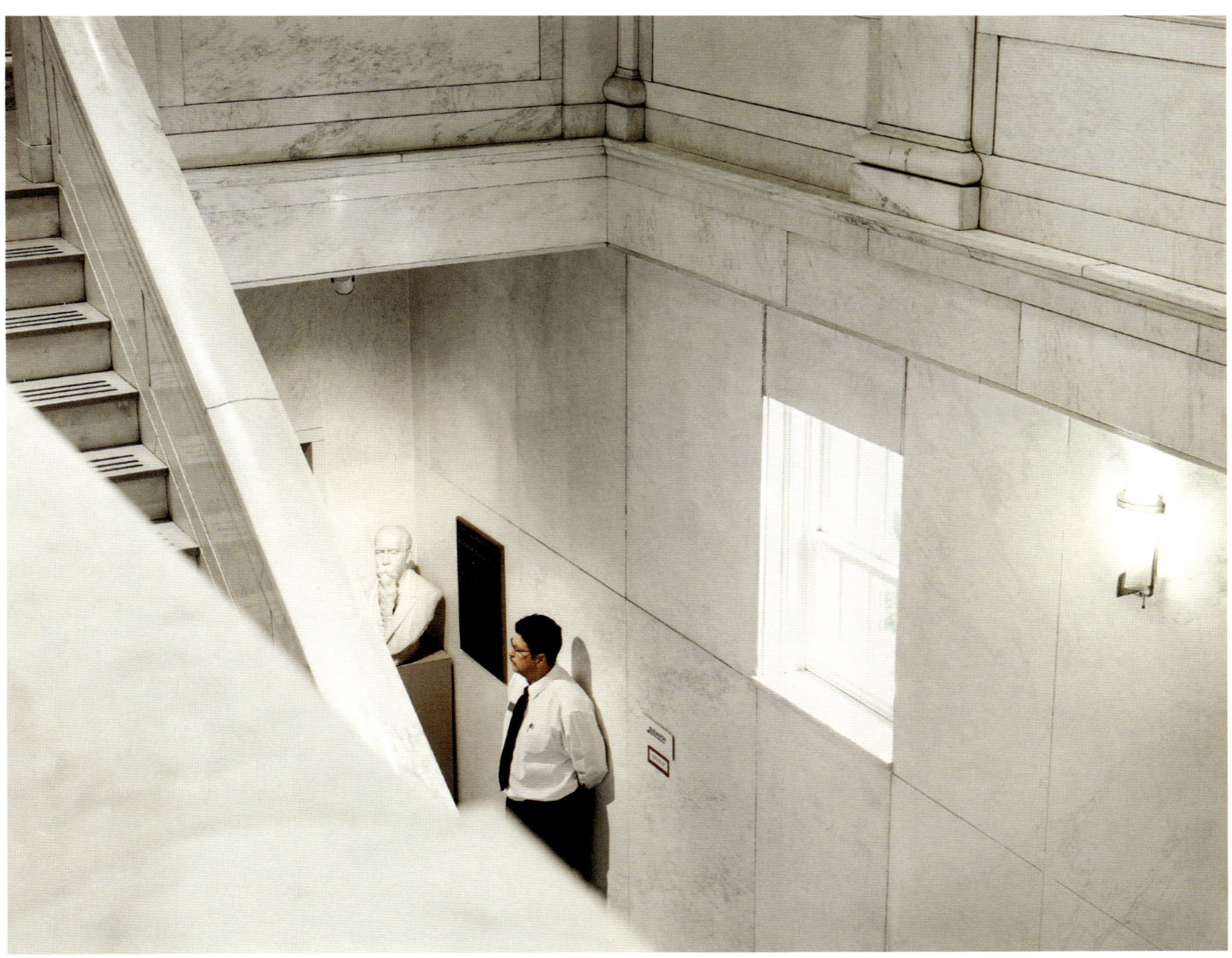

Sausalito Ferry
Sausalito, California

Ferry Boat Discretionary Program. The Federal Highway Administration received $60 million for the Ferry Boat Discretionary (FBD) Program under the American Recovery and Reinvestment Act. The funds were allocated to build ferry docks and facilities, construct ferry boats, and improve ferry service while saving and creating jobs.

Amount funded by Recovery Act: $3,200,000.00

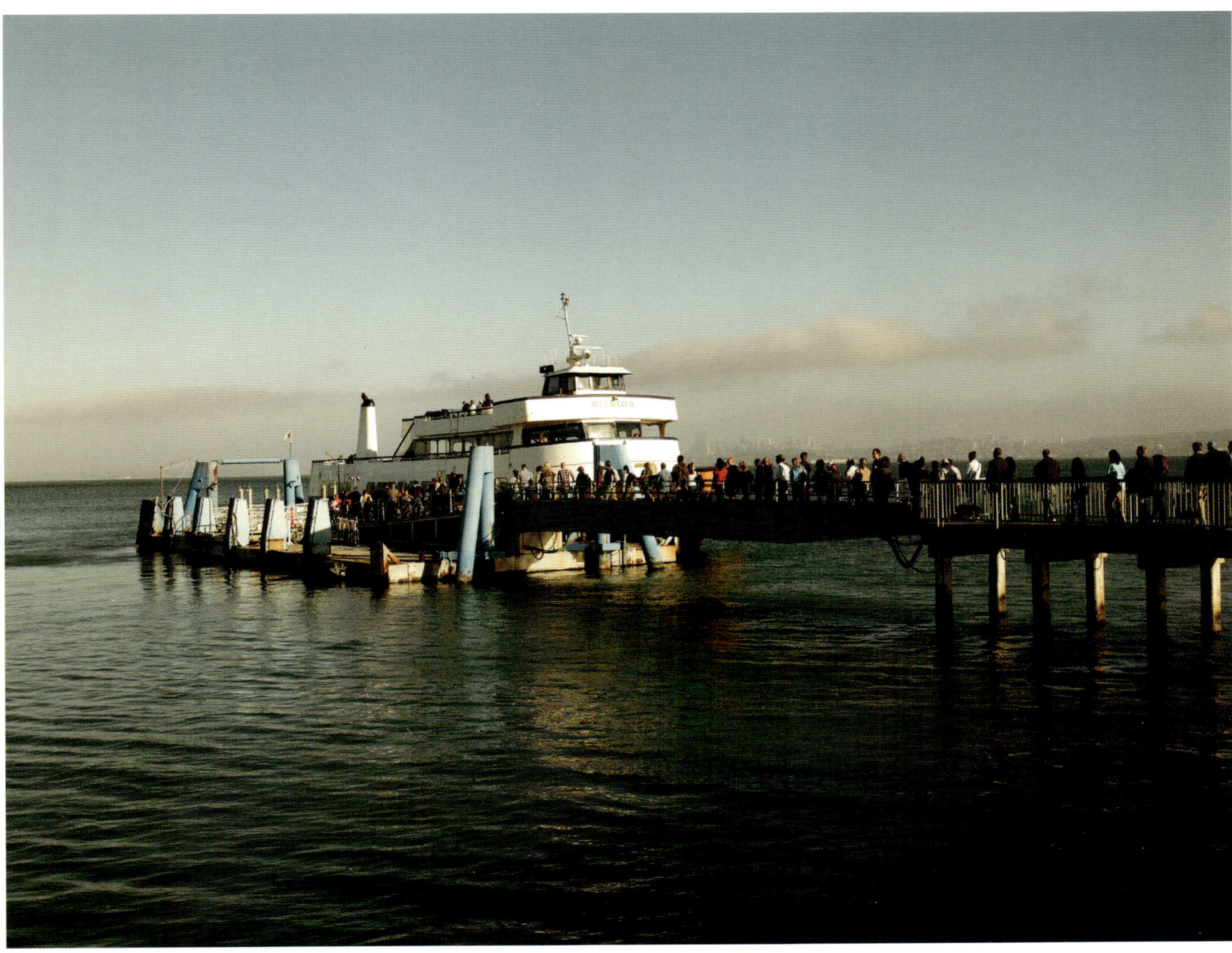

Stearns Park Beach
East Lansing, Michigan
(TWO IMAGES)

The surveillance cameras will be placed in key locations in the
Stearns Park Beach recreation area and in Downtown Ludington.

Amount funded by Recovery Act: $16,782.00

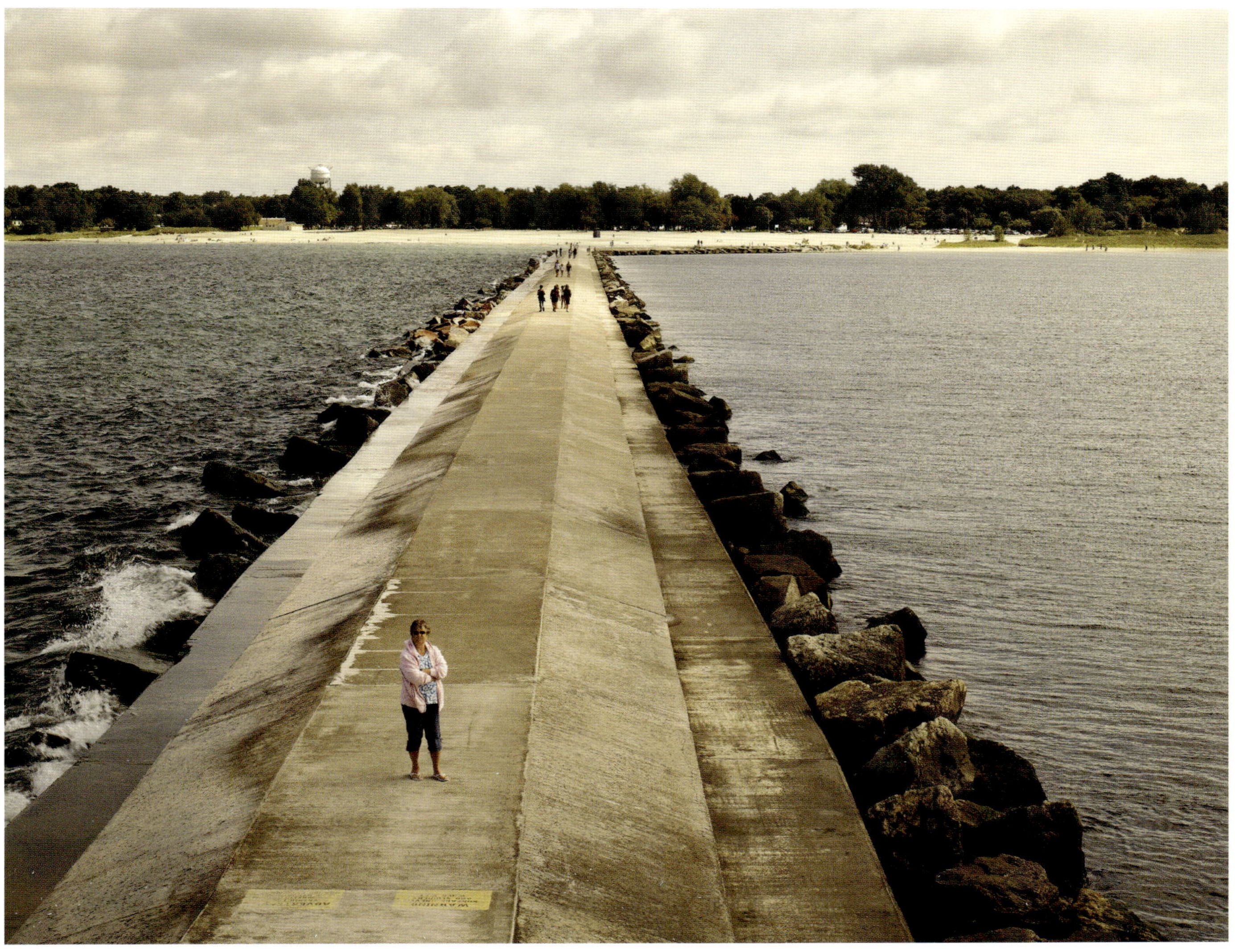

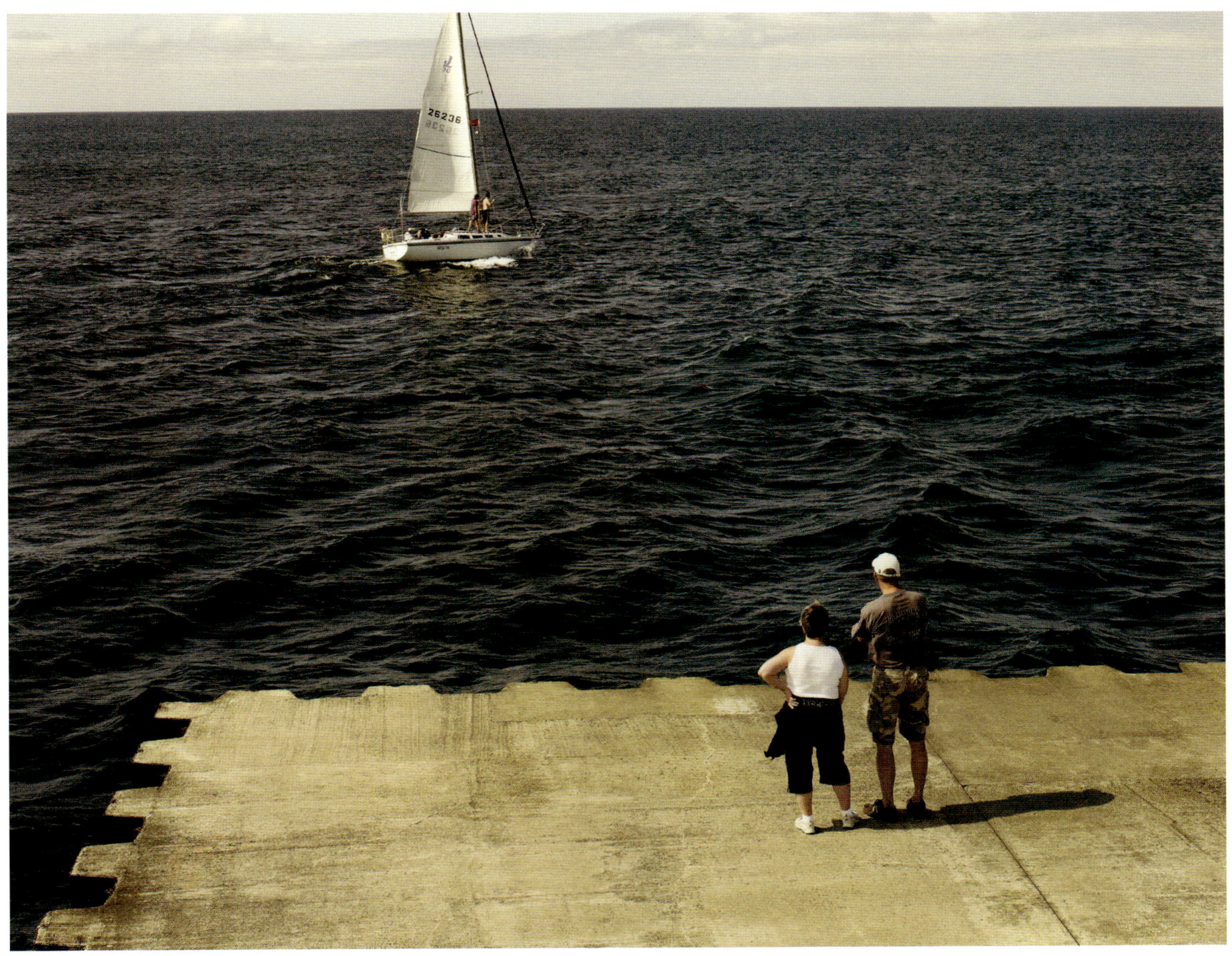

Brownfields
Lincoln Park, Michigan

The City plans to use the grant to develop an inventory of
Brownfields within the Community, and then perform
environmental assessments on priority sites to identify issues of
concern and help prepare them for sale and/or redevelopment.

Amout funded by Recovery Act: $200,000.00

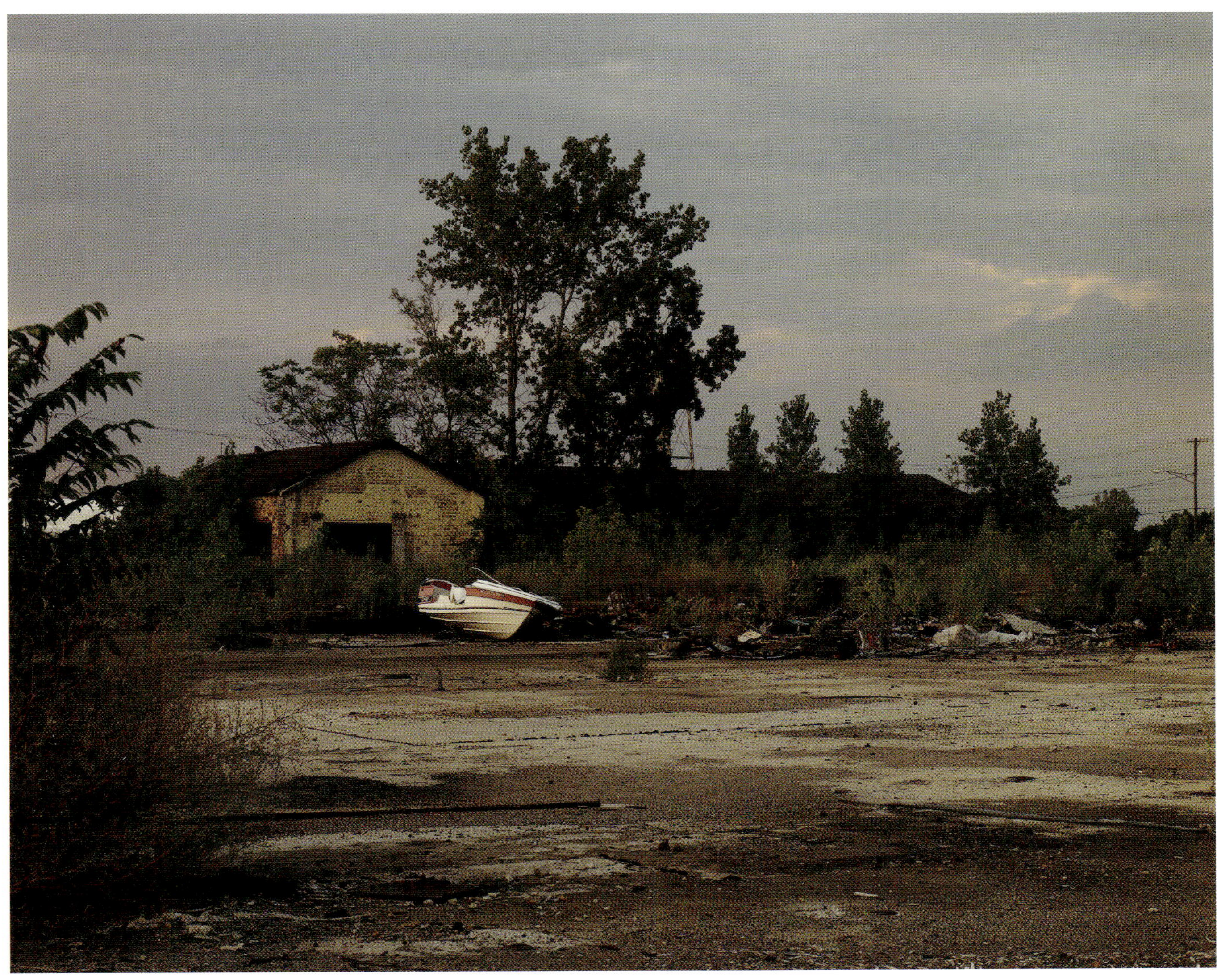

Town of Selma
Selma, North Carolina

Expand on the current library building.

Amount funded by Recovery Act: $100,000.00

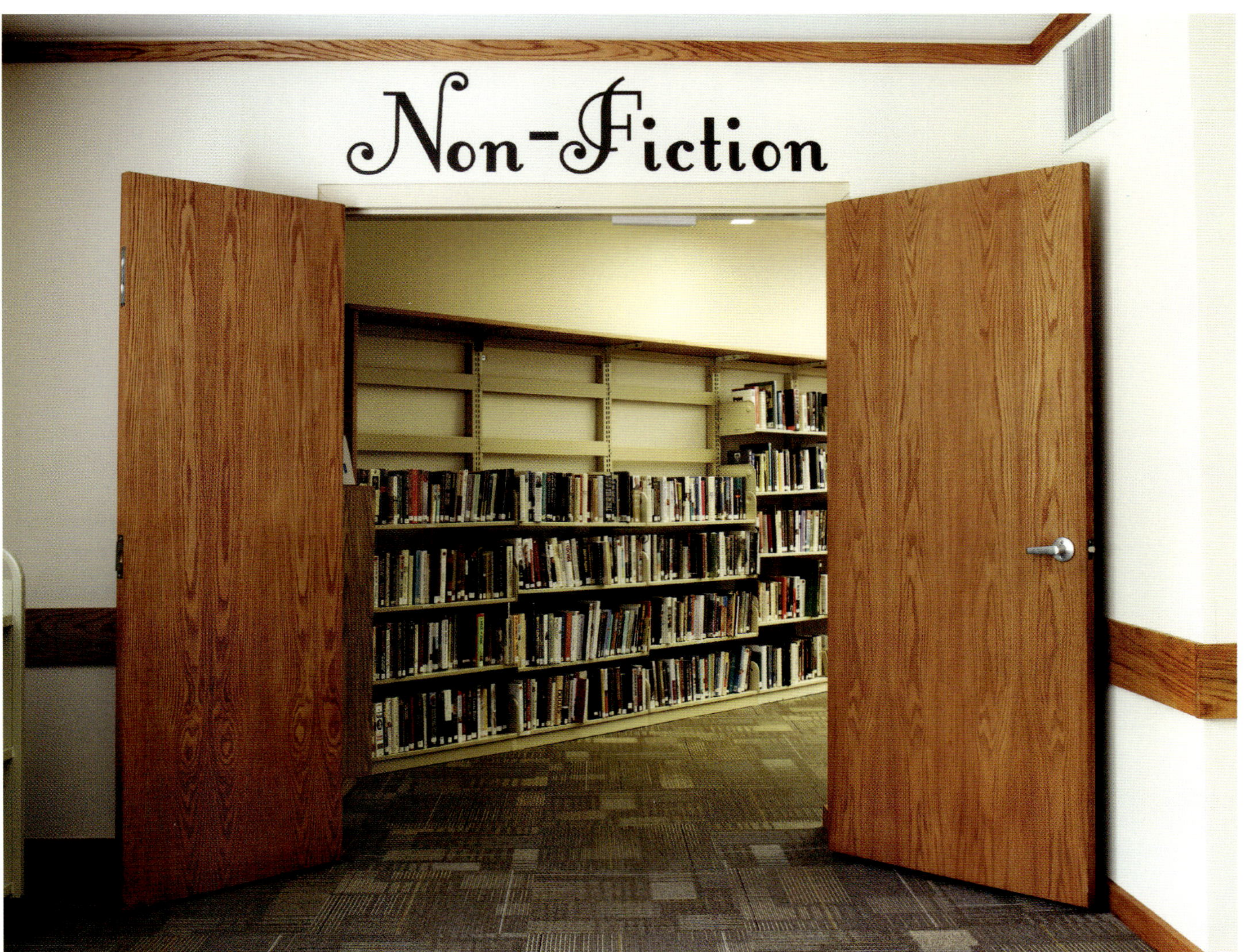
Non-Fiction

From the Infrastructural Sublime to
Not Interesting Enough
Jordan H. Carver

1. A selection of Ress's *America Recovered* images was used to illustrate Volner's essay. Ian Volner, "The Invisible Stimulus: In Search of What Obama Built," *Harper's* (November 2012), 64.

2. Congressional Budget Office, *Estimated Impact of the American Recovery and Reinvestment Act on Employment and Economic Output from October 2011 Through December 2011* (February 2012), 1, http://www.cbo.gov/sites/default/files/cbofiles/attachments/02-22-ARRA.pdf.

3. In a telling May 2013 article, professor and public administrator Paul Posner puts the financial scope of the Recovery Act in context with the New Deal yet focuses on Roosevelt's public popularity and his ability to win broad political support for many New Deal programs. See Paul L. Posner, "The Political Reality of the Stimulus," *Governing: States and Localities*, February 20, 2013, http://www.governing.com/columns/mgmt-insights/col-political-reality-economic-stimulus-obama-roosevelt-decentralized-government.html.

4. Michael Grabell, *Money Well Spent? The Truth behind the Trillion-Dollar Stimulus, the Biggest Economic Recovery Plan in History* (New York: Public Affairs Books, 2012).

5. Michael Grunwald, *The New New Deal: The Hidden Story of Change in the Obama Era* (New York: Simon & Schuster, 2013).

6. Robert D. Leigninger "The Legacy of New Deal Space," *Journal of Architectural Education* vol. 49 no. 4 (May 1996): 226.

7. Federal Works Administration, *Final Report on the WPA Program, 1935-1943* (Washington, DC: Government Printing Office, 1946), 52.

8. Both remarks on New Deal style from Leigninger, "The Legacy of New Deal Space," 228.

9. David E. Nye, *American Technological Sublime* (Cambridge: MIT Press, 1994).

10. Burke's categorical definition of "power" can be applied here to both the state and the aesthetic practices used to represent it: "Besides these things which directly suggest the idea of danger, and those which produce a similar effect from a mechanical cause, I know of nothing sublime which is not some modification of power. And this branch rises as naturally as the other two branches, from terror, the common stock of everything that is sublime." See Edmund Burke, *A Philosophical Enquiry* (Oxford: Oxford University Press, 1990), 59.

11. Robert O. Self, *American Babylon: Race and the Struggle for Postwar Oakland* (Princeton: Princeton University Press, 2003), 13–14.

12. *American Recovery and Reinvestment Act of 2009*, Pub. L. No. 111-5, https://www.gpo.gov/fdsys/pkg/BILLS-111hr1enr/pdf/BILLS-111hr1enr.pdf.

13. Sharon Otterman, "Republicans are Resistant to Obama's Stimulus Plan," *New York Times*, January 25, 2006, http://www.nytimes.com/2009/01/26/us/politics/26talkshow.html. "Economist: Obama Stimulus Not Enough," *CBS News*, December 28, 2008, http://www.cbsnews.com/news/economist-obama-stimulus-not-enough.

14. Rancière's defines "aesthetic practices" as: "'aesthetic practices' as I understand them, that is forms of visibility that disclose artistic practices, the place they occupy, what they 'do' or 'make' from the standpoint of what is common to the community." Jacques Rancière, *The Politics of Aesthetics: The Distribution of the Sensible*, trans. Gabriel Rockhill (London: Continuum, 2004), 13.

15. Rancière, *The Politics of Aesthetics*, 13.

16. US House of Representatives, *Analysis of the First Year of the Obama Administration: Public Relations and Propaganda Initiatives* (August 16, 2010), 26.

17. Text taken from a cached version of the website on the Internet Archive Wayback Machine. See, "Recovery.gov," Internet Archive Wayback Machine, accessed June 26, 2018, https://web.archive.org/web/20091202002357/http://www.recovery.gov/Pages/home.aspx.

18. US House, *Analysis of the First Year*, 26.

19. Recovery.org is no longer active. ProPublica, a non-profit journalism organization has compiled their own database using the same data released by the government. According to ProPublica, there is no data available after October 2012. See "Recovery Tracker," ProPublica, October 1, 2012, http://projects.propublica.org/recovery.

20. Suzanne Mettler, *The Submerged State: How Invisible Government Policies Undermine American Democracy* (Chicago: University of Chicago Press, 2011), 1.

21. "America Recovered: A Survey of the ARRA," Chad Ress personal website, accessed November 12, 2016, http://www.chadress.com/americarecovered.

22. Sianne Ngai, *Our Aesthetic Categories: Zany, Cute, Interesting* (Cambridge: Harvard University Press, 2012), 119.

23. Sianne Ngai, "Merely Interesting." *Critical Inquiry* vol. 34, no. 4 (2008): 777-817.

24. Ngai, *Our Aesthetic Categories*, 136.

25. In an interview with *Cabinet Magazine* Ngai states, "judgments like 'interesting' seem to demand justification, much in the same way that all aesthetic judgments (including even 'interesting') demand concurrence. The justification of aesthetic judgments, which will always involve an appeal to extra-aesthetic judgments—political, moral, historical, cognitive, and so on—is, I think, the really interesting

heart of all aesthetic discourse and experience." Adam Jasper and Sianne Ngai, "Our Aesthetic Categories: An Interview with Sianne Ngai," *Cabinet Magazine* 43, (2011), http://www.cabinetmagazine.org/issues/43/jasper_ngai.php.

26. Adam Jasper and Sianne Ngai, "Our Aesthetic Categories: An Interview with Sianne Ngai."

27. Ngai describes the use of bureaucratic systems and information as an "aesthetic of information." Ngai, "Merely Interesting," 792.

28. Toby Jurovics, "Same as it Ever Was: Re-Reading New Topographics," in *Reframing the New Topographics*, eds. Greg Foster-Rice and John Rohrbach (Chicago: The Center for American Places at Columbia College Chicago, 2010), 1.

29. Britt Salvasen, "New Topographics," *New Topographics* (Göttingen and Tucson, AZ: Steidl and Center for Creative Photography, 2009), 11.

30. Quote and description from John Rohrbach, "Introduction," in *Reframing the New Topographics*, xiv.

31. William Jenkins, "Introduction," in *New Topographics: Photographs of a Man-altered Landscape* (Carlisle, MA: Pentacle Press, 1975), 5.

32. Salvesen, *New Topographics*, 44.

33. Taken from "Prologue" in *New Topographics* (2009), 9.

34. Note taken from Rohrbach's introduction. This essay was also mentioned in Selvesen's essay. Charles Demarais, "Topographical Error," *Afterimage* vol. 3, no. 5 (1975): 10–11.

35. Ngai, *Our Aesthetic Categories*, 168.

36. Jenkins, *New Topographics* (1975), 5.

Taking Stock:
Chad Ress's Photographs of the Recovery Act
Miriam Paeslack

1. Andrew Hinderaker, "Chad Ress—America Recovered," *TIME*, June 25, 2011, http://time.com/3778454/chad-ress-america-recovered.

2. Jan Estep, "Picture Making Meaning: An Interview with Jeff Wall," *Bridge Online* 2, (September 2003).

3. "About," Chad Ress personal website, accessed August 3, 2017, http://www.chadress.com/read-me-2.

4. Keendall L. Walton, "Transparent Pictures: On the Nature of Photographic Realism." *Critical Inquiry* vol. 11, no. 2 (December, 1984), 254.

5. Walton's theory is used here as a general entry point into thinking about fiction and photography and is not intended to stand in for a comprehensive philosophical assessment of his approach. See a critical review of his approach in Derek Matravers, *Fiction and Narrative* (Oxford: Oxford University Press, 2014).

6. "But photography's various other talents must not be confused with … its remarkable ability to put us in perceptual contact with the world, an ability which can be claimed even by a … badly exposed snapshot depicting few details and offering little information. It is this—photography's transparency—which is most distinctively photographic and which constitutes the most important justification for speaking of 'photographic realism.'" See Walton, "Transparent Pictures," 273.

7. In conversations relating to this work.

8. Section 1521 of the American Recovery and Reinvestment Act of 2009 called and described the responsibilities of a "Recovery Accountability and Transparency Board" in order to "coordinate and conduct oversight of covered funds to prevent fraud, waste, and abuse." See *American Recovery and Reinvestment Act of 2009*, Pub. L. No. 111-5, https://www.gpo.gov/fdsys/pkg/BILLS-111hr1enr/pdf/BILLS-111hr1enr.pdf.

9. Ress, "About."

10. Ress's body of work joins a trend in data-visualization artworks that typically seek to render large public data sets interpretable and thereby accessible. These include projects like theyrule.net by Josh On, the work of Laura Kurgan at her Center for Spatial Research at Columbia University, and others.

11. Hinderaker, "Chad Ress."

12. Yoko Ono's *Grapefruit* & John Cage's notational experiments are also significant here.

13. Sol LeWitt, "Paragraphs on Conceptual Art," *Artforum*, June 1967.

14. See, Diamuid Costello and Margaret Iversen, "Photography after Conceptual Art," *Art History* vol. 32, no.5 (December 2009). See also Jeff Wall's texts on the subject. Jeff Wall "'Marks of Indifference'; Aspects of Photography in or as Conceptual Art," in *Reconsidering the Object of Art 1965-1975*, eds. Ann Goldstein and Anne Rorimer (Los Angeles: Museum of Contemporary Art, 1995), 247-267; and Jeff Wall, "Conceptual, Postconceptual, Nonconceptual: Photography and the Depictive Arts" *Critical Inquiry* vol. 38, no. 4 (Summer 2012), 694-704.

15. "America Recovered: A Survey of the ARRA," Chad Ress personal website, accessed August 3, 2017, http://www.chadress.com/americarecovered.

16. Hinderaker, "Chad Ress."

17. The FSA's photography program was active between 1935 and 1944.

18. See Stryker's letter to Frederick P. Soule regarding Dorothea Lange. Roy Stryker to Frederick P. Soule, *Dorothea Lange Itinerary, California and Southwest,*

December 6, 1935, Library of Congress, Farm Security Administration/Office of War Information Written Records: Selected Documents, https://www.loc.gov/rr/print/coll/fsawr/12024-2-Co5-D2-1p. See also the letter defining the script approach. Roy Stryker to John Fischer, *Request from Region 12 for the services of a photographer and suggestion on a proposed film strip*, January 14, 1938, Library of Congress, Farm Security Administration/Office of War Information Written Records: Selected Documents, https://www.loc.gov/rr/print/coll/fsawr/12024-4-FS38-D1-2p.pdf.

19. Sean O'Hagan, "New Topographics: Photographs That Find Beauty in the Banal," *The Guardian*, February 8, 2010, https://www.theguardian.com/artanddesign/2010/feb/08/new-topographics-photographs-american-landscapes.

20. "Glossary," Tate, 2005, http://www.tate.org.uk/whats-on/tate-modern/exhibition/jeff-wall/resources/jeff-wall-glossary; Karen Rosenberg, "Jeff Wall," *New York Times*, January 12, 2012, https://www.nytimes.com/2012/01/13/arts/design/jeff-wall.html. See also Hilde van Gelder's extensive exploration of this concept and related issues of the vernacular and classicism in photography. Hilde van Gelder, "The Shape of the Pictorial in Contemporary Photography," *Image & Narrative* vol. 10, no.1 (2009), http://www.imageandnarrative.be/inarchive/Images_de_linvisible/Vangelder.htm.

21. Hans-Ulrich Obrist, *Do it: The Compendium* (New York: Independent Curators International, 2013).

22. See "Mike Gotch Memorial Bike and Pedestrian Bridge Dedication," Pacific Beach Town Council, April 26, 2012, http://www.pbtowncouncil.org/2012/04/mike-gotch-memorial-bike-and-pedestrian-bridge-dedication.

23. Timothy Keegan, "W.P.A. Construction in San Francisco (1935-1942)," Found SF, 2003, http://www.foundsf.org/index.php?title=W.P.A._Construction_in_San_Francisco_(1935-1942).

24. *The New West, Photographs by Robert Adams*, foreword John Szarkowski (New York: Aperture Press, 2008), 9.

25. Wall's *The Storyteller* (1986) demonstrates the shared compositional sensitivities between Ress's *Rose Creek Bridge* and Wall's work. It also reveals their fundamentally different intentions. The Storyteller, a protagonist in the photograph of a hill beneath a highway and seated in the lower left corner and gesticulating toward her two listeners, Wall explains, is an allegorical image. It "expresses the historical crisis of the Native peoples of Canada, whose traditions of oral history have been eroded by modern life." He underlines this position when he remarks, "I like the fact that when you really look at the world, conceptual oppositions collapse, or become much more complex. You realise that the concrete overpasses are neither majestic sculptures nor hideous, oppressive monoliths. They're just spaces that we experience in different ways." Quoted in "Room 4: *The Storyteller* 1986," Tate, 2005, http://www.tate.org.uk/whats-on/tate-modern/exhibition/jeff-wall/room-guide/jeff-wall-room-4.

26. Arthur Lubow, "The Luminist," *New York Times Magazine*, February 25, 2007, http://www.nytimes.com/2007/02/25/magazine/25Wall.t.html.

27. Helen Machado, "Recovery Funds Help Los Angeles River," website of Representative Lucille Roybal-Allard, April 28, 2009, https://roybal-allard.house.gov/news/documentsingle.aspx?DocumentID=131507.

28. "Fort Peck Dam, Montana," Metropolitan Museum of Art, http://www.metmuseum.org/art/collection/search/265299.

29. Ben Cosgrove, "LIFE's First-Ever Cover Story: Building the Fort Peck Dam, 1936," *TIME*, November 16, 2012, http://time.com/3764198/lifes-first-ever-cover-story-building-the-fort-peck-dam-1936.

30. "'Boysville' Closing After 66 Years," *The Tecumseh Herald*, June 16, 2014, http://www.tecumsehherald.com/content/'boysville'-closing-after-66-years.

31. Ress, "About."

32. This water was to come from water previously diverted into the Rio Grande system by Public Law 87-843 of 1962 from water in the Colorado River basin via the San Juan-Chama Project across the Continental Divide. Construction began in 1965. Impoundment of water in Cochiti Lake began in 1973. See, "Cochiti Dam," *Wikipedia*, accessed June 26, 2018, https://en.wikipedia.org/w/index.php?title=Cochiti_Dam&action=history.

33. Szarkowski, *The New West*, 8.

34. Ress, "About."

35. Joel Snyder, "Territorial Photography," in *Landscape and Power*, ed. W.J.T. Mitchell (Chicago: University of Chicago Press, 1994), 175. This essay focuses on photography of the American West of the period between the 1850s and 1880s.

36. On the topic of maintenance in architecture see also, Hilary Sample, "Maintenance Architecture," *Praxis* 6 (2004), 114–121; David Gissen, "From Urban Nature to the Maintenance Environment," in *Manhattan Atmospheres* (Minneapolis: Minnesota University Press, 2013).

37. Ian Volner, "The Invisible Stimulus: In Search of What Obama Built," *Harper's* (November 2012), 66.

38. Hinderaker, "Chad Ress."

39. Ibid.

40. Statistical data about Recovery.gov during the time of its operation between 2009 and 2016 is available through the Internet Archive Wayback machine. See, "Host: recovery.gov," Internet Archive Wayback Machine, accessed July 28, 2017, https://web.archive.org/details/http://recovery.gov.

41. Hinderaker, "Chad Ress."

42. Megan Garber, "The Tao of Shutterstock: What
Makes a Stock Photo a Stock Photo?" *The Atlantic*, May
18, 2012, https://www.theatlantic.com/technology/
archive/2012/05/the-tao-of-shutterstock-what-makes-
a-stock-photo-a-stock-photo/257280.

43. Garber, "The Tao of Shutterstock."

44. Hinderaker, "Chad Ress."

45. The author and literary scholar Kenneth Goldsmith
has coined the term of "uncreative" writing. He
asks whether techniques traditionally thought to
be outside the scope of literature, including word
processing, databasing, identity ciphering, and intensive
programming, can inspire the reinvention of writing.
See, Kenneth Goldsmith, *Uncreative Writing: Managing
Language in the Digital Age* (New York: Columbia
University Press, 2011).

Image Credits

p. 18: Courtesy Library of Congress, Prints &
Photographs Division, FSA/OWI Collection, LC-
DIG-fsa-8a00075.

p. 19: Courtesy National Archives, photo no. 519837,
79-AAB-1.

p. 22: Courtesy National Archives, photo no. 135-SAP-
0710B.

p. 26: Courtesy Vidor, Wikimedia Commons, Public
Domain.

p. 37: © Chad Ress, courtesy the artist.

p. 40: © Chad Ress, courtesy the artist.

p. 40: Courtesy California Historical Society; OV
917.9461 Un38r_002.

p. 41: © Robert Adams, courtesy Fraenkel Gallery, San
Francisco.

p. 41: © Robert Adams, courtesy Fraenkel Gallery, San
Francisco.

p. 43: © Chad Ress, courtesy the artist.

p. 43: © *LIFE* magazine, courtesy Getty Images. Photo
© Margaret Bourke-White.

p. 46: © Chad Ress, courtesy the artist.

p. 46: © The Dorothea Lange Collection, the Oakland
Museum of California. Gift of Paul S. Taylor.

p. 48: © Chad Ress, courtesy the artist.

p. 48: © Estate Bernd & Hilla Becher, represented by
Max Becher, courtesy Die Photographische Sammlung/
SK Stiftung Kultur – Bernd und Hilla Becher Archive,
Cologne.

p. 49: © Lewis Baltz Trust, courtesy Gallery Luisotti,
Santa Monica, California.

p. 51: Screenshot Getty Images, Recovery Act stock
photographs, Getty Images.

Jordan H. Carver

Jordan H. Carver is a writer and educator based in New York. He is a Henry M. MacCracken Doctoral Fellow in American Studies at New York University, managing editor of *Theory & Event*, and a co-organizer of Who Builds Your Architecture? He is the author of *Spaces of Disappearance: The Architecture of Extraordinary Rendition* (Urban Research, 2018) and editor of *Preservation is Overtaking Us* by Rem Koolhaas and Jorge Otero-Pailos (GSAPP Books, 2014). Jordan is a founding co-editor of the *Avery Review*, the 2014–2015 Peter Reyner Banham Fellow at the University at Buffalo, and a 2015 MacDowell Colony Fellow. He is currently working on a historical investigation of race, politics, and the architectures of US-Mexico boundary formation.

Bonnie Honig

Bonnie Honig is Nancy Duke Lewis Professor of Modern Culture and Media (MCM) and Political Science at Brown University. She is the author of several books in democratic theory, most recently, *Public Things: Democracy in Disrepair* (Fordham University Press, 2017). Her article, "The President's House is Empty" (*Boston Review*), went viral when it was published on Inauguration Day, in January 2017. She is currently finishing a book called *Repertoires of Refusal* (fc Harvard University Press).

Miriam Paeslack

Miriam Paeslack's research spans European and North American urban imagery and culture from the nineteenth to the twenty-first century. Trained as an art historian and historian of law in Germany, Italy, and the United States, she specializes in the analysis of visual representations of urban spaces and concepts of architectural and urban memory, heritage, and cultural identity. Paeslack is the author of *Constructing Imperial Berlin: Photography and the Metropolis* (University of Minnesota Press, 2018); and editor of *Ineffably Urban: Imaging Buffalo* (Ashgate, 2013). Her essays and research are published in journals such as *Future Anterior*, the *Journal of Architecture*, and *Fotogeschichte*. She is associate professor of modern and contemporary visual culture and arts management at the University at Buffalo (SUNY).

Chad Ress

Chad Ress was born in Louisville, Kentucky and lives in Ojai, California. Ress works in both documentary and commercial photography. Recent clients include *Harper's Magazine*, *New York Times*, MIT's *Technology Review*, Toyota, Liberty Mutual, Ford, and the Surfrider Foundation. His work has been recognized in *Photo District News*, *American Photography*, *Communication Arts*, The International Photography Awards, The Forward Thinking Museum, The One Show, D&AD Awards, The Cannes Advertising Festival, and Center: Review Santa Fe. Ress recently completed a fellowship with the Center for Social Cohesion at Arizona State University and in conjunction with the New America Foundation. The resulting archive of images documents where Americans go to find a sense of community and connection to place.

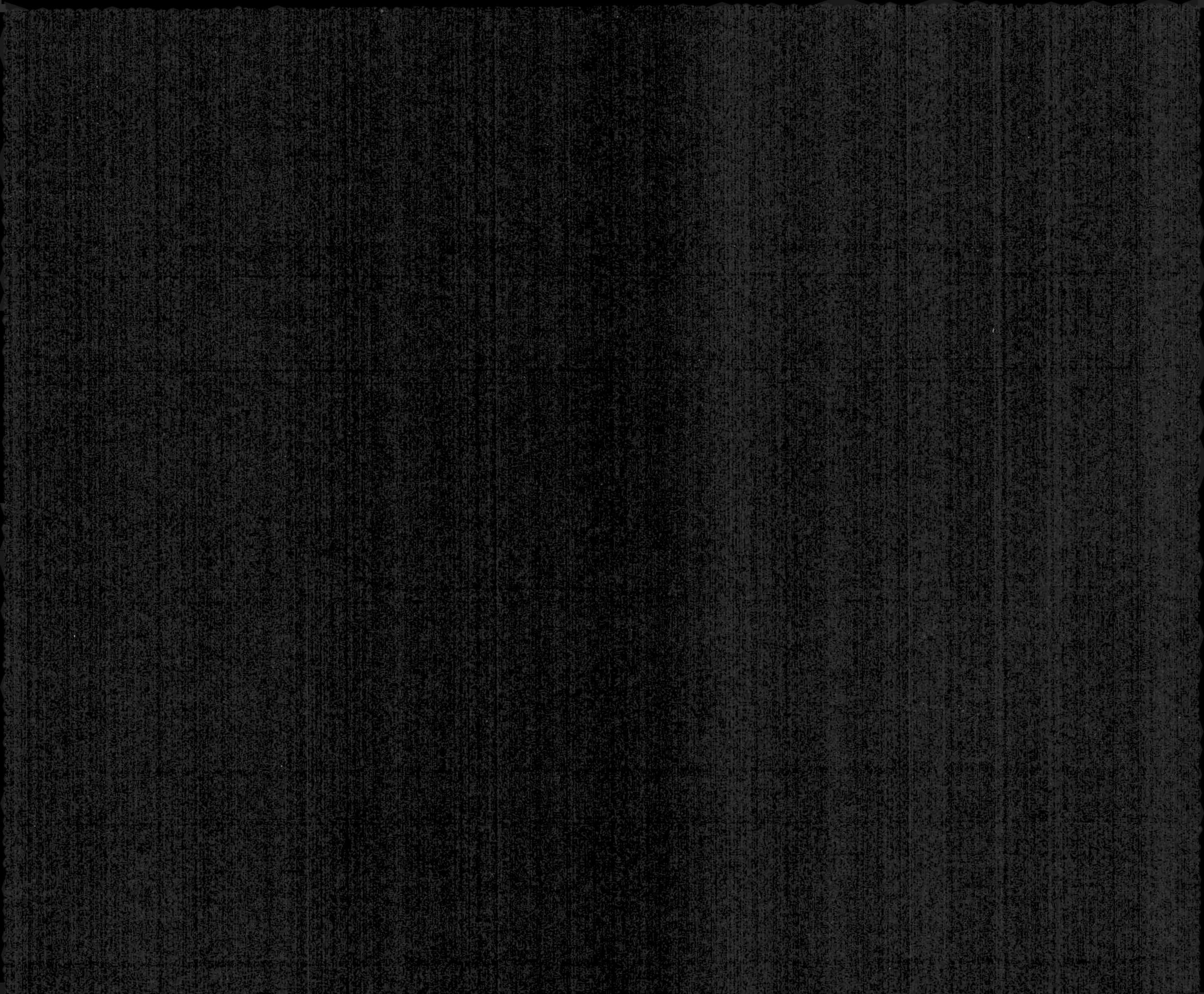